DUDEN

Wissen • Üben • Testen

Englisch

7./8. KLASSE

Dudenverlag
Berlin

Bildnachweis:

Bundesanstalt für Straßenwesen: S. 75
luma_art / shutterstock.com: S. 75 (Rauchen verboten)

Redaktionelle Leitung: Juliane von Laffert
Redaktion: Dr. Stephanie Kramer

Autorinnen: Annette Schomber, Birgit Hock, Dr. Stephanie Kramer,
Dr. Anja Steinhauer (Zeitenübersicht Verben Aktiv/Passiv)
Sprecher: Alison Ripier, Michael Shiels
Tonstudio: CON MOTO GmbH, Ludwigshafen

Herstellung: Ditte Hoffmann
Layoutidee: Lilli Messina, Berlin
Illustration: Carmen Strzelecki
Umschlaggestaltung: 2issue, München
Umschlagabbildung: Thomas Gilke
Layout / technische Umsetzung: Ludger Stallmeister, Wuppertal

www.duden.de
www.cornelsen.de

1. Auflage, 1. Druck 2023

© 2023 Cornelsen Verlag GmbH, Berlin

Das Werk und seine Teile sind urheberrechtlich geschützt. Jede Nutzung in anderen als den gesetzlich zugelassenen Fällen bedarf der vorherigen schriftlichen Einwilligung des Verlages. Hinweis zu §§ 60a, 60b UrhG: Weder das Werk noch seine Teile dürfen ohne eine solche Einwilligung an Schulen oder in Unterrichts- und Lehrmedien (§ 60b Abs. 3 UrhG) vervielfältigt, insbesondere kopiert oder eingescannt, verbreitet oder in ein Netzwerk eingestellt oder sonst öffentlich zugänglich gemacht oder wiedergegeben werden. Dies gilt auch für Intranets von Schulen.

Das Wort **Duden** ist für den Cornelsen Verlag GmbH als Marke geschützt.

Druck: H. Heenemann, Berlin

ISBN 978-3-411-72125-2

PEFC zertifiziert
Dieses Produkt stammt aus nachhaltig bewirtschafteten Wäldern und kontrollierten Quellen.
www.pefc.de

Lösungen und Audiodateien online

Die Audiotracks und die Lösungen zu diesem Heft findest du im Internet.

Geh auf: www.duden.de/wissen-ueben-testen/englisch

Dort kannst du dir die PDFs und die MP3s herunterladen.

Klasse 7

Track	Hörübung	Seite
1	Kapitel 1: Substantive und Artikel – Übung 9	16
2	Kapitel 2: Pronomen – Übung 3	26
3	Kapitel 3: Adjektive – Übung 5	41
4	Kapitel 4: Die Zeiten – Übung 13	60
5	Kapitel 5: Modale Hilfsverben – Übung 3	77
6	Kapitel 5: Modale Hilfsverben – Übung 7	80
7	Kapitel 6: Bedingungssätze – Übung 1	88
8	Kapitel 6: Bedingungssätze – Aufgabe 14	105
9	Kapitel 7: Weitere Nebensatzarten – Übung 4	108
10	Kapitel 7: Weitere Nebensatzarten – Übung 5	109
11	Kapitel 8: Englisch lernen – Übung 13	127
12	Kapitel 8: Englisch lernen – Übung 14 und 15	128
13	Kapitel 8: Englisch lernen – Übung 16 und Aufgabe 7	129, 137

Klasse 8

Track	Hörübung	Seite
1	Kapitel 1: Das Passiv – Übung 8	147
2	Kapitel 2: Die indirekte Rede – Übung 4	168
3	Kapitel 4: Satzverkürzungen – Übung 7	199
4	Kapitel 5: Texte lesen und verstehen – Übung 15	220
5	Kapitel 5: Texte lesen und verstehen – Übung 16	220
6	Kapitel 5: Texte lesen und verstehen – Übung 17	220
7	Kapitel 5: Texte lesen und verstehen – Übung 18	221
8	Kapitel 5: Texte lesen und verstehen – Übung 19	221
9	Kapitel 5: Texte lesen und verstehen – Aufgabe 5	224

Inhalt Klasse 7

1 Substantive und Artikel

- 1.1 Zählbare und nicht zählbare Substantive ⇨ 10
- 1.2 Der Artikel ⇨ 15
  - Klassenarbeit 1–2 ⇨ 19

2 Pronomen

- 2.1 Die Reflexivpronomen ⇨ 24
- 2.2 Reziproke Pronomen und das Stützwort **one/ones** ⇨ 28
  - Klassenarbeit 1–2 ⇨ 32

3 Adjektive

- 3.1 Vergleiche mit Adjektiven ⇨ 38
- 3.2 Das Adjektiv als Substantiv ⇨ 42
  - Klassenarbeit 1–2 ⇨ 44

4 Die Zeiten

- 4.1 Wiederholung: Das **present tense** und das **past tense** ⇨ 49
- 4.2 Das **present perfect** ⇨ 51
- 4.3 Wichtige unregelmäßige Verben (**irregular verbs**) ⇨ 55
- 4.4 Das **past perfect** ⇨ 57
- 4.5 Das **future** ⇨ 61
- 4.6 Das **simple present** und das **present progressive** zur Wiedergabe der Zukunft ⇨ 64
  - Klassenarbeit 1–3 ⇨ 66

Inhalt Klasse 7

5 Modale Hilfsverben

- **5.1** Modale Hilfsverben im **simple present** ⇨ 74
- **5.2** Modale Hilfsverben im **simple past** ⇨ 76
- **5.3** Formulieren mit modalen Hilfsverben ⇨ 79
  Klassenarbeit 1–2 ⇨ 82

6 Bedingungssätze

- **6.1** Der Bedingungssatz Typ I ⇨ 87
- **6.2** Der Bedingungssatz Typ II ⇨ 92
- **6.3** Der Bedingungssatz Typ III ⇨ 96
  Klassenarbeit 1–3 ⇨ 99

7 Nebensätze und Ergänzungen

- **7.1** Adverbialsätze ⇨ 106
- **7.2** Objektergänzungen ⇨ 111
- **7.3** Temporalsätze ⇨ 113
  Klassenarbeit 1–2 ⇨ 116

8 Englisch lernen

- **8.1** Thematischer Lernwortschatz ⇨ 120
- **8.2** Text- und Hörverständnis ⇨ 123
- **8.3** Wörterbucharbeit ⇨ 130
  Klassenarbeit ⇨ 134

Inhalt Klasse 8

1 Das Passiv

- 1.1 Das Passiv im **present tense** ⇨ 140
- 1.2 Das Passiv im **past tense** ⇨ 146
- 1.3 Das Passiv im **present perfect** und **past perfect** ⇨ 149
- 1.4 Weitere Passivkonstruktionen ⇨ 152
- 1.5 Die Zeitformen des Verbs im Aktiv und im Passiv ⇨ 155
  Klassenarbeit 1–2 ⇨ 157

2 Die indirekte Rede

- 2.1 Die Veränderung der Personal- und Possessivpronomen ⇨ 164
- 2.2 Der Gebrauch der Zeiten ⇨ 166
- 2.3 Die Wiedergabe von Fragen und Befehlen ⇨ 171
- 2.4 Modale Hilfsverben in der indirekten Rede ⇨ 175
  Klassenarbeit 1–3 ⇨ 178

3 Relativsätze

- 3.1 Notwendige und nicht notwendige Relativsätze ⇨ 186
  Klassenarbeit ⇨ 190

Inhalt Klasse 8

Satzverkürzungen

4.1 Satzverkürzungen mit Gerundium ⇨ 193
4.2 Satzverkürzungen mit Infinitivkonstruktionen ⇨ 198
4.3 Satzverkürzungen mit Partizipialkonstruktionen ⇨ 201
   Klassenarbeit ⇨ 205

Texte lesen und verstehen

5.1 Sachtexte ⇨ 208
5.2 Texte zusammenfassen ⇨ 213
5.3 Literarische Texte ⇨ 217
5.4 Hörverstehen ⇨ 219
   Klassenarbeit ⇨ 222

Englisch sprechen

6.1 Präsentieren ⇨ 225
6.2 Argumentieren ⇨ 231
   Klassenarbeit 1–2 ⇨ 234

   Stichwortfinder ⇨ 239

WISSEN • ÜBEN • TESTEN

Englisch

7. KLASSE

Wissen

1 Substantive und Artikel

1.1 Zählbare und nicht zählbare Substantive

Zählbare Substantive (Nomen)

Die regelmäßigen Pluralformen der **zählbaren Substantive** *(countable nouns)* werden durch Anhängen von **-s** gebildet.

a friend – a lot of friend**s**
my pencil – those pencil**s**

Achtung: Endet ein Substantiv auf **-s, -ss, -sh** oder **-ch,** wird **-es** angehängt. Die Aussprache ist dann [ɪz].

one bus – four bus**es**
a watch – their watch**es**

Besonderheiten der Schreibweise im Plural:
- Nach einem **Konsonanten** wird **-y** zu **-ies,** nach einem **Vokal** bleibt **-y** erhalten.
- Bei Substantiven auf **-f / -fe** wird der Plural meist auf **-ves** gebildet.
- Einige Substantive auf **-o** haben im Plural **-oes.**

family – famil**ies**, baby – bab**ies**
Aber: boy – boy**s**
shelf – shel**ves**, knife – kni**ves**
Aber: roof – roof**s**, chief – chief**s**
pota**to** – pota**toes**, toma**to** – toma**toes**
Aber: pho**to** – pho**tos**, radi**o** – radi**os**

Nicht zählbare Substantive

Nicht zählbare Substantive *(uncountable nouns)* kommen nur im Singular vor. Sie stehen mit unbestimmten Mengenangaben.

I need **some** water. There is **no** butter in the fridge. My friend usually has **a little** sugar in her tea.

Will man sie zählbar machen, muss ein zählbares Substantiv hinzugefügt werden.

four cups of tea, a slice of bread, six bottles of water

Merke: **Getränke** werden oft zu zählbaren Substantiven, wenn sie zum Beispiel in einem Restaurant bestellt werden.

Two coffees, please. *(statt:* two cups of coffee)
Could I have a beer, please? *(statt:* a glass of beer)

Aufgepasst: Einige Substantive, die nicht zählbar sind, haben auch eine zählbare Form. Die zählbare Form hat dann jedoch eine **andere Bedeutung.**

Your **hair** *(Frisur)* looks lovely today.
There are some **hairs** *(einzelne Haare)* on your shirt.

Do you like **sport** *(Sport)*?
My favourite **sports** *(Sportart)* is tennis.

Wissen

1 Substantive und Artikel

Gruppenbezeichnungen

Gruppenbezeichnungen *(collective nouns)* können sowohl im Singular als auch im Plural gebraucht werden:

family, club, group, class, band, team, crew, army	My family **has / have** already arrived.
Im Singular wird die Gruppe als **Ganzes** betont; steht der Plural, sind die **Einzelnen** in der Gruppe gemeint.	The band **is / are** putting its / their instruments away. **Is / Are** Mr Clark's class difficult to teach?

Es gibt Gruppenbezeichnungen, die immer mit dem **Plural** gebraucht werden:

people – die Leute *the police* – die Polizei *cattle* – Vieh, Rinder	There were only a few people in the shop. The police have just caught the thief. The cattle are hungry.
Achtung: People als zählbares Substantiv hat eine andere Bedeutung.	Are they a peace-loving people *(ein friedliebendes Volk)*? The peoples of Africa *(die Völker Afrikas)* speak different languages.

Einige Substantive haben keinen Singular. Sie kommen nur im **Plural** vor.	clothes – stairs – looks – thanks
Pronomen und Verben, die mit diesen Pluralwörtern kombiniert werden, werden ebenfalls im Plural benutzt.	Clothes *(die Kleidung)* are really cheap here. These stairs *(diese Treppe)* lead to my room. Her looks *(ihr Aussehen)* haven't changed.

Paarwörter

Für Dinge, die aus zwei gleichen Teilen bestehen, verwendet man ein Substantiv im Plural.	trousers – shorts – leggings – tights – jeans – scissors – pyjamas – glasses – headphones
Diese **Paarwörter** *(pair nouns)* stehen immer im Plural und können deshalb niemals mit dem unbestimmten Artikel oder mit Zahlen verwendet werden.	I have bought new jeans. Your pyjamas are great. Where did you get them?
Sie werden mit Verben in der Pluralform verbunden. Mengenangaben wie **a / one pair of** oder **two / three … pairs of** machen Paarwörter zählbar.	My father needs a new pair of glasses. Have you packed your two pairs of trousers?

Üben

1 Substantive und Artikel

Übung 1

 Zählbar oder nicht zählbar? Ordne die Gegenstände dem richtigen Feld zu.

zählbar	nicht zählbar

Übung 2

 Paarwörter: Schreibe auf, was die jeweiligen Personen besitzen.

_____
_____
_____
_____
_____

Üben

1 Substantive und Artikel

Übung 3

 Finde passende Mengenangaben zu den nicht zählbaren Substantiven.

> ~~sugar~~ – sand – money – meat – soup – bread – ketchup – water – butter

a pound of sugar, _____

_____

_____

Übung 4

 Lies die Sätze und unterstreiche die richtige Form.

Do you really want to wear a jeans / some jeans / a pair of jeans?

Many / Much thanks for your help.

Where is / are my pyjamas? – I think I've already packed them / it.

£15 for a pair of scissors / a scissors! It is / They are really expensive.

Übung 5

** Vervollständige die Sätze mit den richtigen Substantiven, Verbformen und Pronomen.

I can't find my 👓 _____ . Have you seen _____ ?

– Yes, here they _____ (to be).

The 🪜 _____ in that house _____ (to be) dangerous. – I know, _____ (to be) very old and almost broken.

Look at that accident over there. We should call 👮👮 _____ .

– Okay, I'll call _____ .

The ✂ _____ you lent me _____ (not to cut) very well.

Your 👱 _____ _____ (to look) great.

Show me your new 👖 _____ . – Here _____ (to be). Do you like _____ ?

🐄 _____ _____ (to be) kept for their milk and meat.

13

Üben

1 Substantive und Artikel

Übung 6

 Finde die Fehler in den folgenden Sätzen und und verbessere sie. Achtung: Drei Sätze sind korrekt!

Do you want coffee?
___

I haven't got a pen.
___

Sarah drinks a water every day.
___

My friends often listen to music when they work.
___

Look at all those hairs on your new anorak.
___

We need a milk and four eggs.
___

Would you like some breads?
___

Übung 7

 Übersetze die folgenden Sätze.

Ich brauche eine neue Strumpfhose und einen Schlafanzug.
___

Es sind heute viele Leute im Park.
___

Trägt Liz gewöhnlich eine Brille?
___

Meine Familie trinkt jeden Tag mehrere Flaschen Wasser.
___

Ich hätte gerne Schokolade und etwas Brot.
___

Wissen

1 Substantive und Artikel

1.2 Der Artikel

Der bestimmte Artikel

Der bestimmte Artikel *(the definite article)* **the** wird benutzt,
- wenn eine **Person** oder eine **Sache** näher bestimmt ist,
- wenn **abstrakte Begriffe** *(life, love, happiness, peace, hate, death)* durch einen Relativsatz oder eine *of*-phrase näher erläutert werden,
- wenn bei Institutionen *(church, school, university, prison)* das **Gebäude** und nicht die Funktion gemeint ist,
- bei **Eigennamen** von Flüssen, Meeren, Museen, Theatern, Hotels, Kinos, Eigennamen mit *of* und Eigennamen im Plural.

The people in our street are very friendly.
We live in the house over there.
The life of Robin Hood was full of adventures.
The love that you can find between them …

She parked her car in front of the school.
The new supermarket is near the church.

the Thames, the Atlantic, the British Museum, the Odeon Cinema, the Hilton Hotel, the Tower of London, the Millers, the Highlands, the Alps

---

Der bestimmte Artikel wird nicht benutzt,
- wenn **abstrakte Begriffe** im allgemeinen Sinn gebraucht werden,
- wenn bei Institutionen die **Funktion** des Gebäudes gemeint ist,
- bei **Eigennamen** von Seen, Gebirgen, Straßen, Parks, Brücken, Plätzen und vielen Gebäuden und Ländern sowie Eigennamen mit Adjektiven,
- bei Monaten, Wochentagen, Feiertagen und Mahlzeiten.

Life can be hard sometimes.
Love makes the world go round.
Most pupils don't go to school on Saturday.
The thieves went to prison for one year.
near Loch Ness, in Bond Street, around Piccadilly Circus, in front of Buckingham Palace, in England, modern Britain, poor Tim
in June, on Tuesday, at Christmas / Easter, after breakfast

Der unbestimmte Artikel

Der unbestimmte Artikel *(the indefinite article)* wird benutzt,
- wenn keine bestimmte Person oder Sache gemeint ist,
- bei Nationalitäten und Berufen,

- bei Verbindungen mit *half, quite, such* und *what*.

Yesterday I met a very nice lady.
They have bought a new car.
Is he an Englishman?
Her mother is a vet *(Tierärztin)*.
half an hour – such a nice boy –
quite a good film – what a lovely day

Üben

1 Substantive und Artikel

Übung 8

Füge den bestimmten Artikel dort ein, wo er nötig ist. Aufgepasst: Oft ist kein Artikel nötig!

I'm thirsty. Where is _____ coke I bought yesterday? – _____ Coke/coke isn't good for you. Why don't you drink _____ water?

_____ Sandwiches/sandwiches you made were fantastic, Kate. I didn't know you could make _____ sandwiches so well.

_____ Life/life in England wasn't easy in the 16th century, not even _____ life of a king or queen.

Sometimes _____ people don't know what is right. _____ People/people who live in our street are usually very loud. _____ People/people can be so unfriendly.

Übung 9

Höre dir Track 1 an und ergänze das fehlende Nomen und den Artikel, falls dieser notwendig ist.

1 _____ that I go to has a lot of pupils. I don't like big schools. Well, I don't like _____ anyway, but my parents think that _____ is important for my future.

Sanjay lives in a big town. There's a prison and a university. Sanjay's sister goes to _____ because she wants to become a doctor. _____ is not far from _____ .

Jim likes football. On his way home from _____ he often plays it with his friends. Last year he broke his left arm playing football and he had to go to _____ . The best thing about breaking his arm was that he didn't have to go to _____ or to _____ . Some of Jim's friends live close to _____ . He sometimes meets them after _____ .

Üben

1 Substantive und Artikel

Übung 10

Vervollständige die Sätze, indem du jeweils einen Satzteil aus dem Wortkasten links und rechts kombinierst.

| what – such – quite | a beautiful dress – an easy question – a lovely meal – a useful thing |

I have never eaten _____.

Look at these clothes. _____.

We can do our homework quickly. It is _____.

A penknife is _____, because you can take it everywhere.

Wissen⁺

Redewendungen mit dem unbestimmten Artikel

Eine Reihe von feststehenden Ausdrücken erfordert immer den unbestimmten Artikel:

*to be in a hurry –
to have a headache / a cold / a temperature –
to take a shower / a bath – to take a seat –
to take a holiday – to make a noise –
for a long time – in a loud voice –
what a pity*

Did you take a shower today?
I haven't been here for a long time.
He doesn't feel well, I think he has a temperature.

Übung 11

Wähle aus dem Wissen⁺-Kasten die richtige Redewendung aus, um die nachstehenden Sätze zu vervollständigen.

Sarah must stay in bed. She _____

Yasmin had a busy day at work. She wants to _____

The Masons' friends came in and _____

"Jeff isn't allowed to come to my party." – _____

Luke was really angry. He said _____ "How dare you!"

Üben

1 Substantive und Artikel

Übung 12

Übersetze die rot markierten Ausdrücke. **The, a / an** oder kein Artikel – entscheide dich.

What did you have zum Frühstück? ⇨ _____

I didn't do anything am letzten Wochenende. ⇨ _____

What would you like zum Mittagessen? ⇨ _____

Where will you spend your holidays im nächsten Sommer? ⇨ _____

Can she visit you im Oktober? ⇨ _____

Let's go to the cinema am Freitagabend. ⇨ _____

Would you like to go swimming am Nachmittag? ⇨ _____

Can we watch a DVD nach dem Abendessen? ⇨ _____

They often go on holiday im Juli. ⇨ _____

Übung 13

Vervollständige die Sätze mit dem bestimmten Artikel, dem unbestimmten Artikel oder lass die Lücke frei.

Who is _____ best player in your team?

Is there _____ supermarket near here? – Yes, it is at _____ end of the street.

Do you live here or are you _____ tourist?

What did you have for _____ breakfast?

Do you play _____ piano?

What time is _____ train to Edinburgh?

Kate never writes _____ letters. She prefers to phone people.

Julia was sick _____ last week, so she couldn't go to _____ school.

Have you ever been to _____ Bond Street?

Last year the Dicksons had _____ wonderful holiday in the north of _____ England.

Testen

1 Substantive und Artikel

Klassenarbeit 1 — 30 Minuten

Aufgabe 1

(*) Ordne die folgenden Substantive der richtigen Zeile zu.

> team – ice cream – glasses – bottle – chocolate – tights – hair – milk – stairs – child – choir – box – sugar – people – cattle – house – beach – jeans – police

zählbare Substantive: _____

nicht zählbare Substantive: _____

Gruppenbezeichnungen: _____

Pluralwörter: _____

Paarwörter: _____

Aufgabe 2

(**) Singular oder Plural? Setze jeweils das richtige Bestimmungswort und/oder die richtige Form der Gegenwart des Verbs in den Klammern ein.

The shorts _____ (to be) new. Tom's trousers _____ (to be) too long.

_____ (This/These) homework _____ (to be) really easy.

The police usually _____ (to come) when you call _____ (it/them). Do you like _____ (this/these) clothes?

Aufgabe 3

(**) Kate war im Supermarkt. Was hat sie alles eingekauft?

Kate has just bought two bottles of

_____

_____

_____

_____

19

Testen

1 Substantive und Artikel

Aufgabe 4

** The, a / an oder kein Artikel – entscheide dich.

Bill takes _____ bath every morning and has cornflakes for _____ breakfast.
Jamila can't go to _____ school today. She has got _____ headache and _____ temperature.
_____ Poor / poor Mr Jenkins. He broke his leg after _____ breakfast.
Sarah is on her way to _____ school. _____ School / school is opposite the museum.
Janice likes music. In _____ afternoons she often plays _____ guitar.
We usually go on holiday in _____ July.
What _____ lovely day! The sun is shining and we can play outside.
Owen wants to become _____ teacher.

Aufgabe 5

*** Übersetze die rot markierten Satzteile ins Englische und schreibe den gesamten Satz richtig auf.

Das Vieh ist in the stable. ⇨ _____
_____

Joe has got drei Jeans. ⇨ _____
_____

Die Treppe ist high. ⇨ _____
_____

Is der Buckingham Palace in London? ⇨ _____
_____

After school I would like to go an die Universität. ⇨ _____
_____

Das Leben can be difficult sometimes. ⇨ _____
_____

Testen

1 Substantive und Artikel

Klassenarbeit 2 — 45 Minuten

Aufgabe 6

Wähle aus dem Wortkasten das richtige Substantiv und schreibe es in der Pluralform in die richtige Lücke.

> coffee – knife – city – bus – story – country – radio – boy – thief – tomato

Some children like reading _____ about ghosts and fairies.

Kevin's friends are from many different _____ all over the world.

London, Paris and Berlin are big _____ .

May we have three _____ , please – without milk.

The _____ are often late these days. I might go by car again.

Those _____ haven't been caught yet.

Here are the _____ to slice the _____ .

The _____ are listening to their _____ .

Aufgabe 7

Entscheide dich für **is** oder **are** in den folgenden Sätzen.

Your hair _____ pretty long.

The police _____ very helpful here.

The bars of chocolate _____ in the cupboard.

The cattle _____ outside.

This band _____ really famous.

The box of toys _____ in Timmy's room.

Testen

1 Substantive und Artikel

Aufgabe 8 ★

Schreibe die folgenden Sätze um, indem du die unterstrichenen Satzteile mit einer **of-phrase** zählbar machst.

May I have some bread please? May I have two _____ ?

How much lemonade do we need? – We need ten _____ .

Let's have some coffee. I'll get us four _____ .

You mustn't forget the soap. Two _____ will be enough.

Aurora likes milk. She has three _____ for breakfast.

Aufgabe 9 ★★

Schreibe dort den bestimmten Artikel vor die Eigennamen, wo er notwendig ist.

_____ United Kingdom   _____ Buckingham Palace

_____ Hyde Park   _____ Pacific Ocean

_____ River Rhine   _____ Jupiter

_____ Odeon Cinema   _____ Ritz

_____ Ground Zero   _____ Great Lakes

_____ Republic of China   _____ M5

Aufgabe 10 ★★

Vervollständige die folgenden Sätze mithilfe des Wortes in Klammern und Präpositionen. Benutze den bestimmten Artikel immer dort, wo er notwendig ist.

Max broke his arm last week. He's (hospital) _____ .

On Sundays our neighbours usually go (church) _____ .

Can we park our car right in front (prison) _____ ?

We have just heard (terrible news) _____ (radio) _____ .

When should teenagers go (bed) _____ ?

Mum is having a shower (bathroom) _____ .

He goes (work / bike) _____ .

Testen

1 Substantive und Artikel

 Bilde Sätze! Benutze dabei die Satzteile aus dem linken und rechten Kasten. Vergiss den bestimmten oder unbestimmten Artikel nicht, wenn dieser notwendig ist.

Aufgabe 11

We arrived at	sea
Have you ever seen	Bond Street
He loves playing	work the teacher gave them
The cyclist was injured and taken to	Euston Station
My friend has	piano
Last year Jeff started to work as	Himalayas
Who fell into	good job
The pupils have just finished	doctor in a hospital
Who was the first man on	hospital
They met in	Moon

Wissen

2 Pronomen

2.1 Die Reflexivpronomen

Formen der Reflexivpronomen

Die **Formen** der Reflexivpronomen *(reflexive pronouns)* enden im Singular auf *-self* und im Plural auf *-selves*.

Singular
I	myself
you	yourself
he, she	himself / herself
it	itself / oneself

Oh dear! I have cut myself.
Did you make the cake yourself?
Dean can repair his bike himself.
She is washing herself.
One might cut oneself.
The dog can open the door itself.

Plural
we	ourselves
you	yourselves
they	themselves

We painted the house ourselves.
Have you hurt yourselves?
They can cook supper themselves.

Aufgepasst: Die Reflexivpronomen werden auf der zweiten Silbe betont.

Gebrauch der Reflexivpronomen

Reflexivpronomen werden folgendermaßen gebraucht:
○ Das Reflexivpronomen **bezieht sich auf das Subjekt eines Satzes zurück:** Das Objekt bezeichnet dieselbe Person wie das Subjekt.
○ Das Reflexivpronomen wird auch verwendet, wenn man ein Nomen oder Pronomen eines Satzes **hervorheben** will.

He cut himself *(sich)* with a knife.
My father is teaching himself *(sich)* English.
Their children can look after themselves *(um sich)*.
The castle itself *(das Schloss selbst, an sich)* is very interesting.
He himself *(er selbst)* was driving.
They spoke to her themselves *(sie redeten selbst mit ihr)*.

Reflexivpronomen stehen in einigen **festen Wendungen**.

Enjoy yourself! – *Viel Spaß!*
Help yourselves! – *Bedienen Sie sich!*
I did it by myself. – *Ich habe es allein getan.*

Üben

2 Pronomen

Übung 1

Setze die richtigen Reflexivpronomen ein.

Mrs Gray hasn't got a teacher. She is teaching _____ French.

He was looking at _____ in the mirror.

I'm not angry with you. I'm angry with _____ .

My parents had a great time in New York. They enjoyed _____ .

We are old enough to look after _____ .

The sandwiches are on the table. Just help _____ , boys.

Übung 2

Was können die Personen nicht selbst machen? Schreibe zu jedem Bild einen Satz und benutze das richtige Reflexivpronomen.

to carry bags

to wash his hair

to repair a bike

to get down

The old lady can't _____ .

_____ .

_____ .

_____ .

Üben

2 Pronomen

Übung 3

Höre dir Track 2 zweimal an und setze die fehlenden Reflexivpronomen ein. Unterstreiche die, die der Verstärkung dienen.

They did the exercises _____.

My brother doesn't want to clean my father's car _____.

Listen! Rita is talking to _____.

I don't know the answer _____. Can you help me, please?

Be careful! You may hurt _____ really badly.

Timmy has made all those sandwiches _____. Isn't he a sweet boy?

Wissen⁺

Reflexives oder nicht reflexives Verb?

Viele Verben, die im Deutschen reflexiv sind, werden im Englischen nicht reflexiv gebraucht:

to apologize – sich entschuldigen	
to be afraid of – sich fürchten	I'm afraid of spiders.
to change – sich ändern	Nothing has changed.
to concentrate – sich konzentrieren	She couldn't concentrate.
to happen – sich ereignen	
to hide – sich verstecken	
to hurry – sich beeilen	Hurry up!
to imagine – sich etwas vorstellen	
to meet – sich treffen	They met in the park.
to move – sich bewegen	Sit down and don't move!
to open – sich öffnen	
to remember – sich erinnern	What happened? – I can't remember.
to sit down – sich setzen	
to wonder – sich fragen	
to worry – sich Sorgen machen	Don't worry.

Üben

2 Pronomen

Übung 4

Lies die Sätze durch, setze das passende Verb in der richtigen Person aus dem Wortkasten ein und entscheide, wann die Verben ein Reflexivpronomen benötigen.

> to help – to enjoy – to hide – to meet – to relax –
> to move – to be afraid

You must be tired. Just _____ and _____.

Are we _____ at 7 o'clock for dinner?

Don't _____. Everything will turn out right.

Look at that tree over there. Its branches are _____ in the wind.

We _____ to some drinks and sandwiches.

Where _____ you _____? I can't see you!

Übung 5

Übersetze die folgenden Sätze ins Englische und benutze, wo nötig, das richtige Reflexivpronomen.

Ich habe dieses Kleid selbst gekauft.
_____

Sei vorsichtig mit der neuen Schere. Du kannst dich schneiden.
_____

Wir müssen uns keine Sorgen machen.
_____

Er beeilte sich, weil er sich im Dunkeln fürchtete.
_____

Anne und Luke haben sich sehr amüsiert.
_____

Wissen

2 Pronomen

2.2 Reziproke Pronomen und das Stützwort **one/ones**

Reziproke Pronomen

Each other und *one another* sind reziproke Pronomen *(reciprocal pronouns)*. Sie werden verwendet, wenn eine Handlung auf **Gegenseitigkeit** beruht.

Bei mehreren Personen kann man statt *each other* auch *one another* verwenden.

Bob and Liz are helping **each other** with their homework.
Do you send **each other** birthday cards?
People often write **one another** on Christmas.

Im Englischen wird unterschieden, ob eine **wechselseitige Beziehung** vorliegt *(each other / one another)* oder ob eine Handlung **reflexiv** ist und sich auf das Subjekt des Satzes bezieht: Dann steht das **Reflexivpronomen** (↗ Kap. 2.1).

Im Deutschen wird in beiden Fällen „sich" übersetzt.

Leila is looking at Ben and Ben is looking at Leila. Leila and Ben **are looking at each other** (= *sie sehen sich gegenseitig an*).

Leila is looking in the mirror. She **is looking at herself** in the mirror (= *sie sieht sich selbst an*).

Das Stützwort *one/ones*

Soll ein zählbares Substantiv nicht wiederholt werden, so kann es durch das Stützwort *(prop-word) one/ones* ersetzt werden.

One steht beim Singular, *ones* beim Plural.

Can I have a new pen? – No, we bought **one** last week.
I've had these shoes for ages. I really need some new **ones**.

Merke: Im Englischen können der bestimmte Artikel oder Adjektive – anders als im Deutschen – nicht alleine stehen. Sie benötigen *one/ones* als Stützwort.

Which of these pullovers do you like best? – The red **one**. *(den roten)*
These T-shirts are nice. – I like the blue **ones**. *(die blauen)*

Üben

2 Pronomen

Übung 6

 Vervollständige die folgenden Sätze und verwende entweder **each other / one another** oder das richtige Reflexivpronomen.

Paul and I live near _____.

You can help Tom and Tom can help you. So you and Tom can help _____.

There's food in the kitchen. If you are hungry, you can help _____.

When we go to the zoo, we always enjoy _____.

Mary and Jamil were at school together but they never see _____ now.

A lot of people talk to _____ when they are alone.

Jill, Mary and Sian are good friends. They know _____ well.

Steve has got a new penfriend. Do they often write to _____?

Mr Benson, I'll do that. I'd like to do it _____.

A lot of children hurt _____ when they get off their bikes too quickly.

Husband and wife should always tell _____ the truth.

Üben

2 Pronomen

Übung 7

Vervollständige die Sätze unten mit den Satzteilen im Wortkasten. Achte auf die richtige Verwendung der reziproken Pronomen und Reflexivpronomen!

look after each other – look after themselves – talk to each other – talk to themselves – help each other – help yourselves

When old friends meet, they often _____.

Young and fit people can _____.

People who live alone often start to _____.

First she was ill in bed, then he was ill, so they had to _____ _____.

Fred and Sheila phone every day to _____ with their homework.

Please _____. Everything you need is on the table.

Übung 8

Vervollständige die Sätze, indem du das Stützwort **one / ones** benutzt.

Can you lend me your pen? – I'm sorry, I haven't got _____.

Which trousers do you like? These _____ or those _____?

Those shoes are much nicer than the blue _____.

Wissen⁺

Das Stützwort **one / ones** kann in folgenden Fällen **entfallen:**

○ nach dem Superlativ eines Adjektivs,

○ nach Ordnungszahlen,

○ nach einem Demonstrativpronomen,

○ nach *any, another, either, neither, each*,

○ nach *which*.

This shirt is the most expensive (one).
Were you the first (one) to arrive?
I think this poster is nicer than that (one).
There are five dogs. Each (one) likes dog biscuits.
We have all these colours. Which (one) do you like?

Üben

2 Pronomen

Übung 9

Entscheide, wann in der folgenden Übung das Stützwort **one / ones** notwendig ist. Wenn du es weglassen kannst, klammere es ein.

Which _____ would you like: the expensive sunglasses or the cheap _____ ?

Which of the two cities is the bigger _____ : London or New York?

My dog is the nicest _____ in the world.

I'm going to buy this _____ , not that _____ .

How many fish did you catch? – I caught three big _____ .

Linda was the third _____ to come in time.

My little sister got a rabbit for her birthday. It's a black _____ .

My brother has got three cats. Each _____ is cute.

Would you like the black one or the white one? – Both _____ , please.

Übung 10

Findest du die Fehler in den folgenden Sätzen? Wenn du sie entdeckt hast, schreibe den korrigierten Satz noch einmal vollständig auf.

Which apples shall we buy? The red?

_____

I have just met Sian in town. We haven't seen ourselves for ages.

_____

Jamil is carrying heavy parcels, but Terry is carrying heavier.

_____

How many towers did this skyscraper have? – I think it had two identical one.

_____

George writes Terry, and Terry writes George. So they write.

_____

Testen

2 Pronomen

Klassenarbeit 1 — 30 Minuten

Aufgabe 1

Fülle die Lücke entweder mit einem Reflexivpronomen oder einem reziproken Pronomen.

Look at your hand. You have cut _____ with the knife.

Billy and Jeff don't do anything together. I don't think they like _____ .

Tom and Jade always help _____ with the washing-up.

How was the concert? Did you enjoy _____ , Tyra?

Some people like talking about _____ all the time.

He did it by _____ .

Aufgabe 2

Setze das richtige Pronomen ein. Achtung: Manchmal darf keines stehen! Lasse die Lücke dann leer.

Billy doesn't have a Spanish teacher. He is teaching _____ Spanish.

Jeff and I met _____ in town this morning.

Mila fell off the skateboard and broke _____ her left arm.

You must learn to concentrate _____ .

My parents have known _____ for about thirty years.

I was so tired I had to sit down _____ .

If you arrive late, you must apologize _____ .

The oven is still hot. Don't touch it! You might burn _____ .

Testen

2 Pronomen

In den folgenden Sätzen gibt es Fehler. Markiere sie und verbessere sie in deinem Übungsheft. Aufgepasst: Ein Satz ist richtig!

Aufgabe 3

We are late, so we must hurry ourselves.

Be careful, don't cut you with that bread knife.

Your friends are really nice now. They have changed themselves a lot.

You can't look at each other because the mirror is broken.

My mum always worries when I'm with my friends.

Can I get me a drink?

Entscheide dich für das richtige Pronomen und unterstreiche es.

Aufgabe 4

Friends usually give themselves / each other presents at Christmas.

Anna and I don't see us / ourselves / each other very often.

My brother always cuts his hair – / himself.

Stop talking about you / – / yourself. That's boring.

While Mary and Jamil were talking to each other / themselves they were looking at each other / themselves.

He can't imagine – / himself what might happen next.

Du gehst mit deinem englischen Austauschschüler einkaufen. Vervollständige die Fragen mit **one / ones** und den angegebenen Adjektivpaaren.

Aufgabe 5

green / red – Swiss / French – old / new – brown / white – chocolate / plain

Which cheese should we buy – the _____ or the _____ ?

Which apples shall we get – _____ ?

Which biscuits do you prefer – _____?

Which eggs do you want – _____ ?

Which car belongs to you – _____ ?

Testen

2 Pronomen

Aufgabe 6

 Bilde aus den folgenden Wörtern Sätze. Ergänze das Reflexivpronomen, reziproke Pronomen oder **one(s)**, falls notwendig. Achte auch auf die richtige Satzstellung!

- Cats / to clean / every day

  _____

- Milo / to enjoy / usually / at parties

  _____

- I / not to feel / very well / at the moment

  _____

- Pat and Jill / to understand / without saying anything

  _____

- There / to be / red apple and / a green

  _____

- Sally's friends / to play with / often / a game of cards

  _____

Testen

2 Pronomen

Klassenarbeit 2 — 45 Minuten

Aufgabe 7

Beantworte die folgenden Fragen, indem du in den Antworten ein Reflexivpronomen wählst. Das einleitende Personalpronomen in der Antwort hilft dir dabei.

Who has made these sandwiches? – We have made them _____.

Who will organise the next bring-and-buy sale? – I will organise it _____.

Who has built those sandcastles? – They have built them _____.

Who drives this car? – She drives it _____.

Who arranged the meeting? – He arranged it _____.

Who washed the dirty pullover? – You washed it _____.

Aufgabe 8

Schreibe die Sätze um, indem du das passende Reflexivpronomen verwendest.

Sian has cut her hand with a knife. She has cut _____ with a knife.

They went to Italy without their parents. They went to Italy _____.

I was sitting in that room. There was nobody else. I was sitting _____.

Tina made biscuits and nobody helped her. She made biscuits all _____.

The girls are looking at their reflection in the mirror. They are looking at _____ in the mirror.

The party was great fun. We enjoyed _____.

Testen

2 Pronomen

Aufgabe 9

 Vervollständige die Sätze und benutze **one** oder **ones**.

I couldn't answer the questions in my last exam because there were only difficult _____.

This shop sells cheap jeans. I like the black _____.

There is a French film and a German film on tonight. Let's watch the French _____.

Anne wants to buy some T-shirts for the summer. She wants a green _____ and two red _____.

Leila has got two brothers: An older _____ and a younger _____.

There is strawberry ice cream and chocolate ice cream for dessert. Which _____ would you prefer?

Aufgabe 10

 Unterstreiche das richtige Pronomen in den folgenden Sätzen.

Ben and Fiona must be in love because they look at each other / themselves quite often.

Help yourselves / each other to the coffee and cake.

Pupils in my class often help each other / themselves when an exercise is really difficult.

I write to my penfriend and he writes to me, so we often write to each other / ourselves.

The Smiths cooked a delicious meal for each other / themselves at Christmas.

We are still fit enough to look after each other / ourselves.

Testen

2 Pronomen

 Markiere die Fehler in den folgenden Sätzen und korrigiere die Sätze. Ein Satz ist richtig.

Aufgabe 11

Sit yourself down and relax.
_____

There is a green apple and a red apple. Which ones would you like?
_____

We met ourselves in the zoo.
_____

My granny is all alone and often talks to herself.
_____

Let's write emails to ourselves.
_____

 Übersetze.

Aufgabe 12

Was hat sich letzte Nacht ereignet?
_____

Kannst du dich noch erinnern?
_____

Ich muss mir keine Sorgen machen.
_____

Sie duscht jeden Morgen.
_____

Er denkt nur an sich.
_____

Wir müssen uns mehr Zeit geben.
_____

Wissen

3 Adjektive

3.1 Vergleiche mit Adjektiven

Eine **Gleichheit** wird im Englischen mit der Konstruktion *as* + **Adjektiv** + *as* (*genauso … wie*) ausgedrückt.	Emma is **as** tall **as** Julie. Is New York **as** big **as** London?
Eine **Ungleichheit** wird entweder mit der Konstruktion **Komparativ** + *than* (*… als*) oder mit *not as / so … as* (*nicht so … wie*) ausgedrückt. *Aufgepasst:* **Than** (*als*) und *then* (*dann*) dürfen nicht verwechselt werden!	Windsor Castle is **bigger than** Buckingham Palace. Living in a city can be **more dangerous than** living in the country. Sue's car is **not as / so fast as** Kevin's car. Going by boat is **more interesting than** going by tube. *Aber:* First we saw the Houses of Parliament, **then** Tower Bridge.
Ungleichheit kann auch mit *less … than* (*weniger … als*) ausgedrückt werden. Diese Wendung hat etwa die gleiche Bedeutung wie *not as … as*.	York is **less interesting than** (not as interesting as) London.
Mit dem Ausdruck *the* + **Komparativ** … *the* + **Komparativ** wird im Englischen die deutsche Entsprechung *je … desto / umso* wiedergegeben. *Aufgepasst:* Die Satzstellung ist anders als im Deutschen: Im Englischen lautet sie in beiden Satzteilen **Subjekt + Verb**.	The bigger a car, **the more expensive** it is. (*je größer …, desto / umso teurer …*) The older Sarah gets, the sillier she becomes. (*je älter …, desto / umso alberner …*) The earlier **I get** up the more tired **I am**. Je früher **ich aufstehe**, desto müder **bin ich**.
Um eine **stetige Steigerung** oder eine allmähliche Entwicklung zum Ausdruck zu bringen, verbindet man im Englischen zwei gleiche Komparativformen mit *and*. Die Wiedergabe im Deutschen erfolgt mit „immer" + Komparativ.	Your English is getting **better and better** (*immer besser*). The film got **more and more** exciting (*immer aufregender*).

Üben

3 Adjektive

Übung 1

Sieh dir die Abbildungen an und vergleiche die Gegenstände mit **as … as**.

Box A is _____ box B.

Julie is _____ Liz.

The blue shoes are _____ the yellow ones.

Mrs Miller _____ Mr Jenkins.

„I'm 92."

„I'm 92."

Übung 2

Verbessere die folgenden Sätze, indem du **not as … as** benutzt.

Athens is older than Rome.
Rome isn't as _____ Athens.

My room is bigger than yours.
Your room isn't _____.

You got up earlier than me.
I didn't _____.

We played better than them.
They didn't _____.

I've been here longer than you.
You haven't _____.

Üben

3 Adjektive

Übung 3

Vervollständige die Sätze mit **as** oder **than**.

I don't watch TV as much _____ you.

You can eat more sandwiches _____ me.

My mother feels better _____ she felt yesterday.

Joey isn't as clever _____ he thinks.

Switzerland is smaller _____ Germany.

The boys couldn't wait longer _____ an hour.

Mexico isn't as big _____ Canada.

Übung 4

Vergleiche Jackies Auto mit Amandas Auto mithilfe der Adjektive in den Klammern.

Amanda's car isn't _____ (big) Jackie's. Jackie's car wasn't _____ (cheap) Amanda's. Jackie's car was _____ (expensive) Amanda's. Amanda's car isn't _____ (modern) Jackie's. Jackie's car is _____ (long) and _____ (wide) Amanda's. Amanda's car isn't _____ (quiet) Jackie's. But Amanda's car is _____ (small) Jackie's, so Amanda's car is _____ (easy) to park in town. Jackie and Amanda both like their car.

Üben

3 Adjektive

Übung 5

Tina hat ihrer Freundin Pat aus Schottland eine E-Mail geschrieben. Höre dir Track 3 an und vervollständige Tinas E-Mail.

3

Dear Pat,

Scotland is great, it is _____ (genauso schön wie) Wales.
Yesterday, I went climbing. It was _____ (schwieriger als) I thought. We had to climb up very high, but _____ (nicht so hoch wie) Snowdon. I'm going pony trekking with some of the girls at the weekend. I think pony trekking is _____ (mehr Spaß als) mountain biking. The longer I stay, _____ (desto aufregender) it is to be here in Scotland. And the people here are even _____ (freundlicher als) back home in Wales, but the summers here seem to be _____ (genauso kalt) they are in Wales. I hope your holidays aren't _____ (nicht so langweilig wie) they were last year.

Love, Tina

Übung 6

Übersetze die deutschen Ausdrücke in den Klammern ins Englische.

Oh dear! You are getting _____ (immer dünner).
_____ (je länger) you sleep, _____ (umso müder) you get.
_____ (je müder) you are, _____ (desto schwieriger) it is to get up.
The rain was getting _____ (immer schlimmer).
_____ (je älter) her son gets, _____ (desto schwieriger) he becomes.

Wissen

3 Adjektive

3.2 Das Adjektiv als Substantiv

Im Gegensatz zum Deutschen können Adjektive im Englischen nicht automatisch als Substantive benutzt werden. Im Singular wird ein zusätzliches Substantiv benötigt.	**Der Blinde** (= der blinde Mann) dort drüben braucht Hilfe. ⇨ **The blind man** over there needs help.
Adjektive können im Englischen jedoch als Substantiv verwendet werden, wenn ein *the* vorangestellt wird. Sie bezeichnen dann eine **Gruppe** oder eine **Gesamtheit** von Personen:	**Die Blinden** (= blinde Menschen) brauchen die Hilfe von anderen. ⇨ **The blind** need the help of other people.
the blind, the rich / the poor, the hungry, the old / the young, the sick, the strong / the weak	The rich of New York *(die Reichen / reichen Einwohner New Yorks)* met at the mayor's party. Sometimes the young *(die Jungen / die jungen Leute)* don't understand the older generation. The ambulance takes the injured *(die Verletzten)* to the hospital.
Merke: Das Adjektiv als Substantiv wird wie eine Pluralform verwendet, das heißt, das Verb steht im Plural. Das Adjektiv hat jedoch **kein Plural-s**.	The young **are** usually careless. The blind **go** to special schools.
Sind **einzelne** Personen gemeint, so muss das Adjektiv durch ein Substantiv wie *person, man, boy, girl, woman, people* ergänzt werden.	A blind man stood at the side of the road. The sick woman had to go to hospital. Some rich people help the poor. The two young girls were standing at the bus stop.
Einige Adjektive sind **echte Substantive** geworden und kommen im Singular und im Plural vor. *the individual – individuals* *the native – natives* Sie können eine Gruppe und auch einzelne Personen bezeichnen.	Must we look after the individuals? The natives had to leave their land.

3 Adjektive

Übung 7

Vervollständige die Sätze mit **the** + Adjektiv. Wähle das richtige Adjektiv aus dem Wortkasten.

> injured – rich – sick – old – young

_____ have the future in their hands.

There is a home for _____ in Sasha's road.

The ambulance arrived just in time and took _____ to hospital.

Julia works in hospital. She looks after _____ .

Robin Hood took the money from _____ .

Übung 8

Übersetze die folgenden Ausdrücke ins Englische.

der Kleine _____   ein Kranker _____

die Tote _____   die Verletzten _____

die Schwachen _____   die Große _____

Übung 9

Vervollständige die Sätze, indem du die richtigen Ausdrücke aus dem Wortkasten auswählst und übersetzt.

> ein alter Mann – die Armen – ein Blinder – junge Leute

There are some good programmes for _____ on TV.

_____ was standing at the side of the road with his guide dog.

The car has just hit _____ who was crossing the street rather slowly.

Many people have no idea of the problems _____ in big cities have.

Testen

3 Adjektive

Klassenarbeit 1 — 30 Minuten

Aufgabe 1 ★

Was glaubst du? Formuliere Vergleiche mit den Adjektiven in Klammern.

A geography lesson is _____ (good) an English lesson.
Comics are _____ (interesting) books.
Football _____ (popular) tennis.
Hiking _____ (exciting) cycling.
My mother _____ (tall) me.

Aufgabe 2 ★★

„Je …, desto …" – beende die folgenden Sätze.

The hotter a day, _____ (I / much / drink).
The more words you learn in English, _____ (you / get good / at English).
The more exciting a book, _____ (I / read / long).
The quicker a car, _____ (to be / it / exciting).

Aufgabe 3 ★★

Formuliere eine stetige Steigerung („immer …"). Das Adjektiv in den Klammern hilft dir.

You couldn't speak French well, but now it is getting _____ _____ (good).
Bread was so cheap, but these days it is getting _____ _____ (expensive).
Houses in big cities are getting _____ (high).
Some streets in my town are getting _____ (dirty).

Testen

3 Adjektive

Aufgabe 4

Ergänze bei den folgenden Sätzen das Adjektiv in den Klammern mit einem Substantiv, falls dies notwendig ist.

We should do more for the _____ (poor).

There's a _____ (blind) in our road. She's 16 like me.

The police found a _____ (dead) in the forest.

The two _____ (old) sitting on the park bench live near us.

The _____ (homeless) in London often sleep in the streets.

Some countries have schools for the _____ (rich).

Aufgabe 5

In jedem der folgenden Sätze ist jeweils ein Fehler. Streiche ihn an und verbessere den Satz, indem du ihn neu schreibst.

We saw a blind who went mountain climbing.

_____

Julia is a bit taller then me.

_____

You are getting more and more thin.

_____

Do you think the riches are really happy?

_____

His concert was as well as the last one.

_____

The quicker a computer, the most expensive it is.

_____

My bike is older as yours.

_____

In the past, olds and youngs all lived together.

_____

Testen

3 Adjektive

Klassenarbeit 2 — 60 Minuten

Aufgabe 6

Vervollständige die Tabelle mit der jeweils richtigen Steigerungsform der Adjektive.

dark		
	sillier	
		best
intelligent		
	worse	
hot		
		quietest

Aufgabe 7

Wähle aus dem Wortkasten das richtige Adjektiv und setze es in der richtigen Steigerungsform mit **than** in die passende Lücke.

big – tidy – expensive – easy – good – friendly – exciting

The flats in Bond Street are _____ those in Oxford Street. It's amazing what one has to pay there.

Look at my room. It's _____ my brother's. His room looks like a dustbin.

Is London _____ Berlin? – I have no idea, but London has about 9 million people, doesn't it?

Testen

3 Adjektive

Our new neighbours are _____ our old ones. They often look after our cats when we are away on holiday.

Dan thinks German is _____ French. – Well, that's just because he has got an A in German. His German is fantastic. It is definitely _____ his French.

The last Superhero film was _____ the first one. I almost fell asleep when I watched the first Superhero film.

---

* Bilde mit den folgenden Satzteilen Sätze mit **as … as**.

Mr Smart's car / old / Mr Miller's car

_____

Scotland / beautiful / Wales

_____

My grandparents / nice / your grandparents

_____

tennis / popular / football

_____

French / difficult / English

_____

My brother / tall / your brother

_____

Aufgabe 8

Testen

3 Adjektive

Aufgabe 9

 Bilde jeweils Sätze mit den Satzteilen aus der rechten und linken Spalte. Benutze den Superlativ des Adjektivs.

The Mona Lisa	busy time of the year
Ben Nevis	hot month
Christmas	famous painting in the world
That was	popular tourist attraction in Scotland
July is usually	good meal I have ever eaten
Loch Ness	high mountain in Great Britain

_____
_____
_____
_____
_____
_____

Aufgabe 10

 Übersetze.

Die Armen brauchen unsere Hilfe.
_____

Die Reichen leben in dieser Gegend.
_____

Der Kranke wurde ins Krankenhaus gebracht.
_____

Die Jungen wollen nichts mit den Alten zu tun haben.
_____

Die Junge könnte freundlicher sein.
_____

Wissen

4 Die Zeiten

4.1 Wiederholung: Das **present tense** und das **past tense**

Das *present tense*

Das *simple present* steht, wenn etwas regelmäßig, häufig, oft, nie oder auch immer geschieht.
Signalwörter: *always, never, often, sometimes, usually, on Mondays, every weekend*

I often **get up** early in the morning.
He never **walks** to school.
They usually **go** to school by bus.

Es steht
○ bei Berufen, Hobbys oder typischen Fähigkeiten,
○ bei der Inhaltswiedergabe und aufeinanderfolgenden Handlungen,

○ bei *when-* und *if-*Sätzen.

My mother is a vet *(Tierärztin)*. Joe swims in his free time.
The story is about a young girl. She lives in London. – First he comes home, then he unlocks the door. Finally he watches TV.
If you don't run, you will miss your bus.

Mit dem *present progressive* wird eine Handlung beschrieben, die im Augenblick des Sprechens gerade abläuft oder noch nicht abgeschlossen ist.
Signalwörter: *at the moment, just, now, still, right now*

Look. It **is raining**.
Sally **is** still **reading** a magazine.
They **are** just **having** tea.
We **are doing** our homework at the moment.

Aufgepasst: Verben der **Sinneswahrnehmung** stehen normalerweise nicht in der Verlaufsform.

The soup tastes good. This song sounds fantastic.

Das *past tense*

Das *simple past* beschreibt eine in der Vergangenheit abgeschlossene Handlung. **Signalwörter:** *yesterday, ago,* Zeitangaben mit *last, in 2012*

She **wrote** a letter.
We **went** to the cinema.
My friend **had** a party last week.
Yesterday we **visited** my grandparents.

Das *past progressive* wird verwendet, um ein Ereignis zu beschreiben, das in der Vergangenheit im Verlauf war, als ein neues Ereignis eintrat.

Tom **was doing** his homework when the phone rang.
While the Browns **were working** in the garden, it started to rain.

Üben

4 Die Zeiten

Übung 1

Simple oder **progressive?** – Unterstreiche die richtige Form des **present tense**.

What time do you usually get up / are you usually getting up?

Kim is excited. She is going shopping / goes shopping.

Oh look! It snows / is snowing again.

Liam is still working / still works on his project in geography.

My parents never eat / are never eating in a restaurant.

Mae sometimes takes / is sometimes taking the dog for a walk.

Übung 2

Lies dir die Sätze durch und setze dann das Verb ins **simple past**.

Tanika often loses her purse. She _____ it last week.

We meet our friends every weekend. We _____ them two weeks ago.

I usually buy some magazines every week. I _____ some last week.

We often go to the cinema on Saturdays. We _____ there yesterday.

My grandparents come to see us every Friday. They _____ to see us last Friday, too.

Mum eats an apple every evening. She _____ one last night, too.

Übung 3

★★★ Vervollständige die Sätze mit der richtigen Zeitform des Verbs in den Klammern.

Where's Lisa? – She _____ (still – to write) a letter in her room.

She always _____ (to go) to bed at 9:30 p.m.

While the Dicksons were having a garden party, it _____ (to start) to rain heavily.

If you _____ (to do) the washing-up, your mum will be pleased.

Mia and Ben _____ (to lie) on the beach at the moment.

The bus stopped because two children _____ (to run) across the road.

Wissen

4 Die Zeiten

4.2 Das **present perfect**

Das *present perfect simple*

Das *present perfect simple* wird gebildet aus ***have / has + past participle***.	
○ Die **regelmäßigen** Formen des *past participle* enden wie die regelmäßigen Formen des *simple past* auf **-ed**,	I / you / we / they **have watched** TV. He / she / it **has arrived**. He has **worked**. They haven't **stopped**.
○ die **unregelmäßigen** Formen müssen gelernt werden.	She has **written**. We have **gone**.
Das *present perfect simple* wird verwendet, um auszudrücken, dass eine vergangene Handlung noch **Auswirkungen** auf die Gegenwart hat. Es wird auch für Handlungen verwendet, die **gerade erst abgeschlossen** wurden.	I have cut my finger. It hurts. Look, I have bought a new computer. They have opened the windows. The air is fresher now in here. The bus has arrived. Let's get on it.
Die folgenden **Signalwörter** erfordern den Gebrauch des *present perfect simple*:	
just – gerade, *never* – niemals, *ever* – jemals, *so far* – bisher, *not … yet* – noch nicht, *since / for* – seit (↗ Wissen⁺-Kasten nächste Seite)	The guests have just arrived. Have you ever been to London? – No, I have never been there. Jane hasn't done her homework yet.

Das *present perfect progressive*

Das *present perfect progressive* wird gebildet aus ***have / has + been + present participle***.	I / you / we / they **have been waiting**. He / she / it **has been waiting**.
Es drückt aus, dass eine Handlung oder ein Ereignis **in der Vergangenheit begonnen** hat und bis in die Gegenwart **andauert** (und noch länger andauern kann).	I have been running. I'm out of breath now. Sarah has been cooking lunch. The kitchen is still untidy.
Zu den **Signalwörtern** gehören:	
how long? – wie lange?, *all day* – den ganzen Tag, *the whole month* – den ganzen Monat, *for one hour* – seit einer Stunde	How long has she been swimming? – She has been swimming for two hours.

Üben

4 Die Zeiten

Übung 4

 Beschreibe, was in den Situationen passiert ist. Wähle aus dem Wortkasten das richtige Verb und setze es ins **present perfect simple**.

to tidy their room – to break her arm – to do the washing-up

Caleb and Nathan _____.

Lilly _____.

Liz and Joe _____.

Wissen⁺

Since und for

Since und *for* sind Signalwörter, die mit dem *present perfect* benutzt werden.

Sie zeigen an, wie lange eine Handlung oder Situation gedauert hat.

Aufgepasst: Since zeigt den **Zeitpunkt** an, *for* die **Zeitspanne**. Die deutsche Bedeutung ist beide Male „seit".

I have had my computer for two years.
He has been driving since 7 o'clock.
We have been here for two months.
It has been raining since we arrived.

since ten o'clock – since yesterday – since 2016
for three hours – for two days – for a long time

Üben

4 Die Zeiten

Übung 5

Beantworte die folgenden Fragen mithilfe des Verbs und des Signalworts in den Klammern.

Have you done your homework? – Yes, I _____ (to do – just) it.

Who is that woman? – I don't know. We _____ (to see – never) her before.

Has Mei ever been to London? – Yes, she _____ (to be – already) there.

Where are my keys? – Sorry, but I _____ them _____ (to find – not yet).

Has the train already arrived? – No, it _____ (not to arrive – yet).

Übung 6

Vervollständige die Sätze mit **for** oder **since** und setze das Verb in den Klammern in die richtige Form: **present perfect simple** oder **progressive**? Achtung: Manchmal sind beide Formen möglich!

Jade _____ (to be) at home _____ 5 o'clock.

My grandparents _____ (to live) in England _____ 14 years.

We _____ (to wait) for the bus _____ 20 minutes.

Mr Robertson _____ (not to work) in his office _____ some weeks.

These houses _____ (to be) empty _____ 2010.

Lin _____ (to learn) to play the piano _____ she was six.

Kevin _____ (to have) his bike _____ last Christmas.

Sasha _____ (to know) her friend _____ years.

Üben

4 Die Zeiten

Wissen+

Präsens im Deutschen, *present perfect* im Englischen

Im Deutschen verwendet man das **Präsens,** wenn man ausdrücken möchte, wie lange etwas schon andauert.

Im Englischen dagegen steht bei *since* und *for* nie das Präsens, sondern das ***present perfect (progressive).***

Ich **lese** dieses Buch jetzt schon **seit** einer Woche.

I **have been reading** this book **for** one week now.

Übung 7

 Formuliere die folgenden Sätze um, indem du **for** oder **since** benutzt. Achte wieder auf die richtige Form – **simple** oder **progressive**?

Chloe is in France now. She arrived there four days ago.

She has been in France for four days.

It's raining. It started two hours ago.

It _____ two hours.

Keiran has got a new camera. He bought it in 2021.

He _____.

Dave plays the guitar. He started when he was eight years old.

_____.

Mr Brown is washing his car. He started to wash it at 4 o'clock.

_____.

Übung 8

 Setze die Satzteile zu sinnvollen Sätzen zusammen und schreibe sie in dein Übungsheft.

Andy	hasn't phoned	to Scotland yet.
She	has never stolen	for some days.
My friend	haven't flown	anything in his life.
They	hasn't been to a pub	since last week.
We	have written	six letters so far.

Wissen

4 Die Zeiten

4.3 Wichtige unregelmäßige Verben (irregular verbs)

infinitive	simple past	past participle	deutsche Bedeutung
to be	was/were	been	sein
to beat	beat	beaten	schlagen
to become	became	become	werden
to begin	began	begun	anfangen
to bite	bit	bitten	beißen
to blow	blew	blown	blasen
to break	broke	broken	zerbrechen, kaputtmachen
to bring	brought	brought	bringen
to build	built	built	bauen
to burn	burnt/burned	burnt/burned	brennen
to buy	bought	bought	kaufen
to catch	caught	caught	fangen, erreichen
to choose	chose	chosen	aussuchen, wählen
to come	came	come	kommen
to cost	cost	cost	kosten
to cut	cut	cut	schneiden
to deal	dealt	dealt	handeln
to do	did	done	tun, machen
to draw	drew	drawn	zeichnen
to dream	dreamt	dreamt	träumen
to drink	drank	drunk	trinken
to drive	drove	driven	fahren
to eat	ate	eaten	essen
to fall	fell	fallen	fallen
to feel	felt	felt	fühlen, sich fühlen
to fight	fought	fought	kämpfen
to fly	flew	flown	fliegen
to forget	forgot	forgotten	vergessen
to freeze	froze	frozen	frieren, gefrieren
to get	got	got	bekommen
to give	gave	given	geben
to go	went	gone	gehen, fahren
to grow	grew	grown	wachsen
to have	had	had	haben
to hear	heard	heard	hören
to hide	hid	hidden	verstecken
to hit	hit	hit	schlagen, treffen
to hold	held	held	halten
to keep	kept	kept	behalten
to know	knew	known	wissen, kennen
to lead	led	led	führen
to learn	learnt/learned	learnt/learned	lernen

Wissen

4 Die Zeiten

Wichtige unregelmäßige Verben (irregular verbs)

infinitive	simple past	past participle	deutsche Bedeutung
to leave	left	left	verlassen, abfahren
to let	let	let	lassen, erlauben
to lie	lay	lain	liegen
to light	lit/lighted	lit/lighted	anzünden, leuchten
to lose	lost	lost	verlieren
to make	made	made	machen, tun
to mean	meant	meant	bedeuten, meinen
to meet	met	met	treffen, kennenlernen
to pay	paid	paid	bezahlen
to put	put	put	legen, stellen
to read	read	read	lesen
to ride	rode	ridden	reiten, fahren
to ring	rang	rung	klingeln, anrufen
to rise	rose	risen	steigen, aufgehen
to run	ran	run	rennen, laufen
to say	said	said	sagen
to see	saw	seen	sehen
to sell	sold	sold	verkaufen
to send	sent	sent	schicken, senden
to shake	shook	shaken	schütteln, zittern
to shine	shone	shone	scheinen
to shoot	shot	shot	(er-)schießen
to show	showed	shown	zeigen
to shut	shut	shut	schließen, zumachen
to sing	sang	sung	singen
to sink	sank	sunk	sinken, versenken
to sit	sat	sat	sitzen
to sleep	slept	slept	schlafen
to speak	spoke	spoken	sprechen
to spell	spelt/spelled	spelt/spelled	buchstabieren
to spend	spent	spent	ausgeben, verbringen
to spread	spread	spread	aus-, verbreiten
to stand	stood	stood	stehen
to steal	stole	stolen	stehlen
to swim	swam	swum	schwimmen
to take	took	taken	nehmen, bringen
to teach	taught	taught	unterrichten
to tell	told	told	sagen, erzählen
to think	thought	thought	meinen, denken
to throw	threw	thrown	werfen
to wake up	woke up	woken up	aufwachen
to win	won	won	gewinnen
to write	wrote	written	schreiben

Wissen

4 Die Zeiten

4.4 Das **past perfect**

Das past perfect simple

Das *past perfect simple* wird gebildet aus **had + past participle**.	I/You/We/They **had looked**. He/She/It **had looked**. He **had arrived**. They **hadn't talked**. She **had seen**. We **had thought**.
Für die **regelmäßigen** und **unregelmäßigen** Formen des *past participle* gelten dieselben Regeln wie für die Bildung des *present perfect* (↗ Kap. 4.2).	
Das *past perfect simple* steht fast immer in Verbindung mit dem *simple past*.	Laura couldn't buy anything at the bar because she **had forgotten** her purse.
Es wird verwendet, wenn man sich auf einen **Zeitpunkt** bezieht, der sich **vor einem Ereignis im** *simple past* ereignet hat. Es handelt sich also um ein Ereignis, das noch weiter zurückliegt als die Vergangenheit (= Vorvergangenheit).	I arrived at 7:30 but Laura **had** already **left** the bar at 7 o'clock. Roy couldn't find his purse. Maybe someone **had stolen** it.

Das past perfect progressive

Das *past perfect progressive* wird gebildet aus **had + been + present participle**.	I/You/We/They **had been walking**. He/She/It **had been walking**.
Das *past perfect progressive* wird verwendet, wenn (wie beim *past perfect simple*) ein Ereignis vor einem Zeitpunkt in der Vergangenheit stattgefunden hat.	It started to rain. The hikers **had been walking** for quite some time.
Es drückt aus, dass eine Handlung oder ein Zustand in der Vergangenheit **andauerte**, als ein anderes Ereignis einsetzte. Das einsetzende Ereignis steht im *simple past*.	My bus arrived at 8:45. I **had been waiting** at the bus stop since 8 o'clock.
Wird ein Nebensatz mit **after** *(nachdem)* eingeleitet, steht er im *past perfect*. Im Hauptsatz muss das *simple past* stehen.	After Liz had left school *(Nebensatz)*, she went to America *(Hauptsatz)*.
Wird der Nebensatz mit **when** *(als)* oder **before** *(bevor)* eingeleitet, steht das *simple past*. Im Hauptsatz wird das *past perfect simple/progressive* verwendet.	I had already known Marc *(Hauptsatz)* before I moved to Wales *(Nebensatz)*. Mia had been talking to her friend *(Hauptsatz)* when Ahmed came in *(Nebensatz)*.

Üben

4 Die Zeiten

Übung 9

Vervollständige die folgenden Sätze mit der **past perfect simple-**Form des Verbs in den Klammern.

After we _____ (to buy) the tickets, we went to the concert.

I phoned the police because someone _____ (to steal) my car.

The tourists _____ (to visit) the castle before they went to their hotel.

Joe _____ (not to finish) his homework when Phil phoned.

_____ you _____ (to go) to Bristol before you flew to London?

Übung 10

Die Wilsons waren in Cornwall. Formuliere zu jedem Bild einen Satz, der die vorhergehende Handlung nochmals aufgreift.

1. After the Wilsons had decided to go to Cornwall, they packed their bags.

2. After they had packed _____ , they _____ .

3. _____ ,
   _____ at their hotel.

4. _____
   _____ .

5. _____
   _____ .

Üben

4 Die Zeiten

Übung 11

Mache aus zwei eins: Verbinde die einzelnen Sätze mit **after, when** oder **before.**

Her parents sold their house. They bought a bungalow.
After her parents had sold their house, they bought a bungalow.

Ben graduated from school. He went to university.
_____

The lessons began. The pupils got to school.
_____

The train left. They got to the station.
_____

The thieves left the bank. The police arrived.
_____

I started breakfast. The doorbell rang.
_____

Übung 12

Vervollständige die folgenden Sätze, indem du das **simple past** und das **past perfect simple** in jedem Satz verwendest. Beachte die Reihenfolge der Handlung.

When the ship _____ (to sink), the passengers _____ (to be) at sea for months.

After Anne _____ (to see) a film about King Arthur, she _____ (to want) to read a book about him.

Tim _____ (not to ride) on a horse before he _____ (to spend) a few days on a farm.

When the boys _____ (to arrive) at the café at 12:30, it _____ (to close) half an hour earlier.

The tourists _____ (not to realize) that they _____ (to take) the wrong way.

Üben

4 Die Zeiten

Übung 13

 Höre dir den Text über Cindy auf Track 4 an. Beantworte anschließend die Fragen und achte dabei darauf, dass du die richtige Zeitform wählst.

 What language did Cindy learn after she had learnt French?
4 _____

What did she do when she had learnt Spanish?
_____

What did she want to do after she had taught at her school for three years?
_____

What did she do when she had come back home from Madrid?
_____

Übung 14

 Setze in die Lücken entweder das **past tense**, das **past perfect simple** oder das **past perfect progressive**.

to live / to move: How long _____ you _____ in Europe before you _____ to New York?

to go: He _____ never _____ by Underground before.

to travel: After he _____ for half an hour he realised that he was going in the wrong direction.

to drive: How long _____ Rajesh _____ before he had his first accident?

to talk / to hear: My mother _____ to her neighbour when she suddenly _____ a terrible noise.

to collect / to listen / to acquire: Liam _____ Beatles records for a while before he actually _____ to them. He _____ already _____ quite a few records when he decided to sell them.

Wissen

4 Die Zeiten

4.5 Das *future*

Im Englischen kann man zukünftige Ereignisse mit verschiedenen Zeitformen ausdrücken: dem *going to-future* und dem *will-future*.	I **am going to** spend the summer in Italy. It **will be** hot in Italy in summer.

Das *going to-future*

Das *going to-future* wird gebildet mithilfe der Präsensformen von *be*, dem Ausdruck *going to* und dem Infinitiv des Vollverbs.

We **are going to drive** down to San Diego for the wedding.
I'm not going to eat this.

Es wird verwendet,
- um Pläne und Absichten auszudrücken,
- wenn Dinge oder Ereignisse mit großer Sicherheit eintreten werden.

We are going to travel to Italy in summer.
This is too much ice cream. I am going to be sick.

Das *will-future*

Das *will-future* wird gebildet mithilfe des Wortes *will* und dem Infinitiv (ohne *to*) des Vollverbs.

I **will be** there on time.
I am sure you **will like** the film.

Anstelle von *will* kann häufig auch die Kurzform *'ll* stehen.

I**'ll get** myself something to drink.

Es wird verwendet, um
- allgemeine Vorhersagen,

They will receive many presents for their wedding.

- Vermutungen oder Hoffnungen sowie

I'm sure my mum will help me with the baby.

- spontane Überlegungen auszudrücken.

I'm hungry. I will walk over to the fast food restaurant across the street.

Um Sätze im *will-future* zu **verneinen,** wird ein *not* zwischen *will* und Vollverb geschoben.

My train is already late. I'm sorry, I will not be there on time.

Merke: Die Kurzform von *will not*: **won't**.

I won't sign this letter.

Üben

4 Die Zeiten

Übung 15

Bei Familie Smith klingelt das Telefon. Die Großmutter erkundigt sich nach den Plänen der Familie für den Nachmittag. Verwende das **going to-future**, um die Antworten zu formulieren.

Grace / to read / a book

_____

Anne / to play / in the backyard

_____

Dad / to bake / a cake / for the weekend

_____

Lily / not to do / her homework because she is ill

_____

Übung 16

Sarah und ihre Mutter machen anhand des Wetterberichts im Internet Pläne für die Ferien. Verwende das **will-future**.

Monday   Tuesday   Wednesday

32°C

Sarah: "It _____ (regnen) on Monday. I _____ (bleiben) in bed until noon. I _____ (aufstehen) only to fetch myself something to eat and to drink!"

Sarah's mum: "It _____ (bewölkt sein) on Tuesday. I _____ _____ (dich ausführen) shopping. And we _____ (einladen) your grandparents for dinner."

Sarah: "It _____ (sonnig sein) on Wednesday. I _____ (verbringen) the day at the swimming pool. And maybe I _____ (treffen) Henry there, too."

Mum: "I _____ (sich nicht anschließen), because I don't like swimming pools at all. I _____ (sich entspannen) with a book on the sofa."

Üben

4 Die Zeiten

Übung 17

 Sarah und Henry liegen am Pool. Verwende entweder das **going to-** oder das **will-future**.

Sarah: "I'm hot. I _____ (to get) myself an ice cream over at the cafeteria."

Henry: "Wait! I _____ (to go) with you. I _____ (to get) myself something to drink."

A couple of minutes later …

Sarah: "Let's go back to the others! I _____ (not/to enjoy) my ice cream here!"

Henry: "I _____ probably _____ (to go back) into the water again, soon."

Sarah: "I won't. I _____ (to have to leave) soon."

Henry: "Bye-bye then! _____ (to be) at Tim's party on Saturday?"

Sarah: "Yes, I _____ (to be)."

Henry: "If it is okay I _____ (to pick up/you)?"

Sarah: "Of course. Thank you. I hope it _____ (to be) a good party. See you on Saturday. Bye-bye."

Wissen⁺

Verben mit zukünftiger Bedeutung

In einer Verbindung mit dem Infinitiv eines Vollverbs (= *to* + Verb) haben manche Verben allein von ihrer Aussage her bereits zukünftige Bedeutung. Dazu gehören: *to expect* und *to hope*.

I **expect** her **to pass** the driving test.
I **hope to hear** again from you soon.

Offizielle Ereignisse, die sich in der Zukunft ereignen werden, werden mit *be to* + Infinitiv formuliert.

My mother **is to give** a speech at my brother's wedding.

Wissen

4 Die Zeiten

4.6 Das **simple present** und das **present progressive** zur Wiedergabe der Zukunft

Das *simple present*

Das *simple present* wird zur Wiedergabe der Zukunft verwendet, wenn es sich um einen **feststehenden Termin** handelt, der nicht beeinflussbar ist, wie etwa genaue Zeitangaben, Fahrpläne oder Programme. Deshalb spricht man auch von *timetable future*.

Das *timetable future* wird vor allem bei folgenden Verben gebraucht:

to arrive, to leave, to begin, to start, to end, to open, to close

Our train leaves at four minutes past twelve.
It arrives in Manchester at twenty to three.
When does the concert start?
The guided tour through London ends at 5 o'clock.
This bookshop closes at 10 p.m.

Das *present progressive*

Das *present progressive* drückt aus, dass jemand etwas für die Zukunft **fest geplant** oder **vereinbart** hat.

What are you doing next week? – I'm meeting Kate in the afternoon, but I'm not doing anything special in the afternoon.
Mum, you needn't collect me after Nico's party. Asha's mother is giving me a lift.

Damit es keine Verwechslungen mit dem *present progressive* zur Wiedergabe von gegenwärtigen Handlungen gibt, werden oftmals Zeitbestimmungen der Zukunft verwendet. Zu diesen **Zeitangaben** gehören:

tomorrow, on Thursday, next week, this summer, every weekend

I'm helping Sarah with her homework.
(= Ich helfe ihr gerade.)

Aber: I'm helping Sarah with her homework tomorrow. (= Ich helfe ihr morgen. Es ist vereinbart.)

Üben

4 Die Zeiten

Übung 18

Sieh dir die Termine folgender Personen an und schreibe auf, was sie für die Zukunft geplant haben.

Tim – visit – his granny – 7:30 p.m.

_____

Paul and Linda – in an hour – play – computer games

_____

Silas – write – some letters – tonight

_____

Lin and Ann – tomorrow – go – sports centre – with Eddy

_____

Übung 19

Mrs Gray, die Lehrerin von Ben, erläutert ihrer Klasse die wichtigsten Termine für die Klassenfahrt nach Schottland. Schau dir ihre Notizen an und vervollständige dann den Text mit der richtigen Form der Zukunft.

Monday
bus start – 9:30 a.m.
lunch – 12:30 p.m.
arrive Edinburgh – 6 p.m.

Tuesday
climb Arthur's Seat

Wednesday
Holyrood House – 10 a.m.
bus from Youth Hostel – 3 p.m.

Mrs Gray: "Our trip _____ on Monday 3rd. The bus _____ from the main gate at 9:30 a.m. We _____ lunch at 12:30, and the bus _____ in Edinburgh at about 6 o'clock. On Tuesday we _____ Arthur's Seat. On Wednesday we _____ Holyrood House at 10 a.m. You know that it is a royal palace. Don't forget that the bus _____ from the Youth Hostel at 3 p.m. So don't be late."

Testen

4 Die Zeiten

Klassenarbeit 1 — 60 Minuten

Aufgabe 1 (*)

Vervollständige die Sätze, indem du entweder das **present progressive** oder das **simple present** benutzt.

Sam's grandparents _____ (to live) in Edinburgh.

Listen, Ava! The train _____ (to come)! Hurry up.

My mother _____ (often – to grow) a lot of flowers,

but this year she _____ (not to grow) any.

Aufgabe 2 (*)

Entscheide dich für die richtige Verbform und unterstreiche sie.

What have you been doing / have you done all afternoon?

Have you done / Have you been doing your homework yet?

Joe and I have been sitting / have sat in the kitchen all evening.

Samira hasn't been eating / hasn't eaten anything since lunch.

Someone has stood / has been standing there in the dark for a long time and has watched / has been watching us through the window.

Aufgabe 3 (**)

Bilde Sätze und verwende die richtige Zeit. Das Signalwort hilft dir.

He – just – to go to the dentist
_____

They – to win the World Cup – 2012
_____

Some strange people – to try to open the door – at the moment
_____

I – not to practise my English vocabulary – yesterday
_____

Testen

4 Die Zeiten

 Du blätterst gerade in Noahs alten Notizen. Schreibe auf, was er letzte Woche gemacht hat. Achte auf die richtige Form des **past tense**!

Aufgabe 4

holiday – start – on Sunday
_____

the next day – repair my broken bike
_____

on Tuesday – to go to York by bike
_____

later that day – visit the cathedral
_____

when – cycle home – start to rain
_____

get terribly wet – and take a hot bath
_____

while – watch TV – have my tea
_____

 Bilde Fragen und verneinte Antworten. Entscheide, ob du **present perfect simple** oder **present perfect progressive** benötigst.

Aufgabe 5

Kim / to read / for a long time

Has Kim _____ ?

Kim hasn't _____ .

Ahmed / to take photos / all afternoon

_____ ?

_____ .

Colin and Fred / to play / tennis / since breakfast

_____ ?

_____ .

Testen

4 Die Zeiten

Aufgabe 6

** Lies dir jeweils die Ereignisse durch. Beginne mit dem Satz, der rot markiert ist, und achte auf die richtige Zeitenabfolge in den weiteren Sätzen: **past perfect simple** oder **simple past**?

(1) Somebody broke into the office during night.
(2) We arrived at work in the morning.   (3) We called the police.

We _____ at work in the morning and found that

somebody _____ into the office during night. So we

_____ the police.

(1) Ann went out.
(2) I tried to phone her this morning.   (3) There was no answer.

I tried to phone Ann this morning but _____

no answer. She _____ out.

(1) Kevin came back from London a few days ago.
(2) I met him the same day.   (3) He looked very well.

I _____ Kevin a few days ago. He _____

well. He _____ .

Aufgabe 7

*** Setze die richtige Verbform in die Lücke: **past perfect progressive** oder **past perfect simple**?

Sarah and I were good friends. We _____ (to know)

each other for a long time.

Nala was sitting on the ground. She was tired. She _____

(to run).

When I arrived, everybody was sitting round the table and talking. They

_____ (already – to eat).

Mia was sad when she sold her bike. She _____ (to have)

it for a very long time.

When I arrived, Kate _____ (already – to wait)

for me.

Testen

4 Die Zeiten

Klassenarbeit 2 — 60 Minuten

Aufgabe 8

Das **present tense** oder das **past tense**? Unterstreiche in den folgenden Sätzen die richtige Form.

My friend Stella is going / went / goes to New York last year.

Grandfather broke his arm while he was cycling / cycled / cycles home.

When I see / saw / was seeing him, he was carrying a gun.

Who comes / is coming / was coming to Juliet's party next week?

Baraz is an architect. He enjoys / is enjoying / enjoyed his job.

What does / is / did Anne do / doing / do? I think she is working in the garden.

Aufgabe 9

Beantworte die folgenden Fragen in der jeweils richtigen Zeitform. Verwende in der Antwort das Verb in der Klammer.

What has Lilly just done? She (to write letters) _____.

What did you do last weekend? I (to go shopping) _____.

What have the Millers been doing all morning? They (to play tennis) _____

_____.

What was Harry doing between 7 o'clock and 8 o'clock? He (to phone a friend)

_____.

What have Philip and Nick already done? They (to take the dogs for a walk)

_____.

Aufgabe 10

Bilde aus den folgenden Satzteilen Sätze. Achte darauf, dass du den Infinitiv des Verbs in die richtige Zeit setzt – das Signalwort in der Klammer hilft dir dabei.

Pablo's mum / to cook / Spanish food (since she was a child)

_____

Sam / to teach German (in 2010)

_____

Testen

4 Die Zeiten

Her friend / to be ill (for three days)
_____

His parents / to live / Brighton / to live in Oxford (after)
_____

Bob / to play / for Manchester United (from March to June)
_____

We / to leave for France (tomorrow)
_____

The pupils / to study / in the library (at the moment)
_____

Marisa / to wash her hair / to go to the cinema with Nick (before)
_____

Aufgabe 11

*** Bringe die passenden Satzhälften zusammen – die Signalwörter helfen dir dabei – und schreibe hinter jeden Satz die Zeitform des Verbs.

He flew in a helicopter	for two hours now.
My aunt was making sandwiches	yet.
Milo was a dancer	since yesterday.
My friends have been watching TV	last summer.
Their daughter hasn't learned to swim	from 2004 to 2020.
My dog has been lying under my bed	while she was listening to the radio.

He flew in a helicopter last summer. (simple past)
_____
_____
_____
_____
_____

Testen

4 Die Zeiten

Aufgabe 12

Übersetze die Sätze ins Englische.

Bevor wir Rhea ins Krankenhaus gebracht haben, ist sie vom Rad gefallen.

_____

Es regnet. Zieh deine Gummistiefel (wellies) an.

_____

Tom ist bisher schon zwei Mal umgezogen.

_____

Sie hört sich manchmal die alten Schallplatten an.

_____

Ella und Gavin sitzen immer noch am Computer.

_____

Aufgabe 13

Creative writing. Entscheide dich für eine der Fragen und schreibe drei bis fünf Sätze.

1. What will you do next weekend?
2. What will the weather be like next Christmas?
3. What will you do when you've finished school?

Testen

4 Die Zeiten

Klassenarbeit 3  45 Minuten

Aufgabe 14

Bei der folgenden Aufgabe sind die Zeiten und Verben durcheinander geraten. Setze die unterstrichenen Verbformen in den jeweils passenden Satz.

I <u>was running</u> to Switzerland yet.

My train <u>watched</u> at 7:30 a.m.

The children <u>haven't been</u> a DVD two hours ago.

Hey look! Mrs Green's cat <u>leaves</u> next to the pond.

Chris <u>is sitting</u> through the park last Sunday morning.

Aufgabe 15

Bilde Sätze. Achte dabei auf den richtigen Gebrauch der Zeiten.

My sister Nala / travel / to New York / next Christmas

She / buy / her ticket / tomorrow

Nala / spend / the holidays / with family for the first time.

Her boyfriend / hope / family / not / buy / too many presents / for Christmas

I / expect / my parents / be sad / to celebrate Christmas without her

Testen

4 Die Zeiten

Aufgabe 16

 Schreibe mithilfe der Satzteile in den Wortkästen einen kleinen Text über Liz. Aufgepasst: Du musst das **present perfect** und das **past perfect** jeweils in der **simple-** oder **progressive-**Form verwenden!

live – Manchester – since 2007 / live in England all her life / meet – best friends – Sandra – Jill – Dave – when – join Park School

she – have a penfriend from Germany – for three years / they – write a lot / her penfriend – promise to visit her – but – not visit her yet

after – she – come to Manchester – she – start to play football / she – play football – for some years now

_____
_____
_____
_____
_____

Aufgabe 17

 Überprüfe, ob du das **present perfect** und das **past perfect** richtig verwenden kannst. Achte auf die richtige Übersetzung von „seit"!

1. Andrew lernt seit den letzten Sommerferien Deutsch.
   Bevor Andrew Deutsch gelernt hat, sprach er schon Französisch.
   _____
   _____

2. Unsere Mannschaft hat noch kein Spiel verloren.
   Nachdem wir letztes Jahr einige Spiele verloren hatten, übten wir mehr.
   _____
   _____

3. Wie lange wart ihr unterwegs gewesen *(to be on the road)*?
   Als wir endlich ankamen, waren wir seit mehr als fünf Stunden gefahren.
   _____
   _____

Wissen

5 Modale Hilfsverben

5.1 Modale Hilfsverben im **simple present**

Die Formen der modalen Hilfsverben im *simple present* sind: *can / cannot (can't), may, must, ought to, shall* und *will*. Sie stehen im Satz vor einem Vollverb und ergänzen es um die Aussage, ob etwas getan werden kann, muss, darf oder soll.	You **can** do your homework later. **May** I go to Tom's party tonight, Mum? In summer, you **must** water your flowers twice a day.
Auf ein modales Hilfsverb folgt immer der Infinitiv eines Vollverbs ohne *to*, außer bei *ought to*.	The house **ought to** be painted this summer.
Merke: Modale Hilfsverben haben in der 3. Person Singular kein *-s* und bilden auch keine *-ing*-Form.	He may arrive any time. She can't borrow my car today, I need it myself.
Modalverben sind Hilfsverben und brauchen daher kein anderes Hilfsverb, um Verneinungen oder Fragen zu bilden.	can ⇨ cannot/can't; may ⇨ may not; shall ⇨ shall not; ought to ⇨ ought not to; will ⇨ will not/won't
Aufgepasst: In der Verneinung mit *not* erfährt das Modalverb *must* eine Bedeutungsänderung: *must not / mustn't* heißt *nicht dürfen*.	You must not talk during the lesson. You mustn't watch TV after 10 p.m.
Die modalen Hilfsverben werden folgendermaßen verwendet: ○ *can:* Fähigkeit, Erlaubnis oder Möglichkeit ○ *may:* höfliche Bitte ○ *must:* Pflicht (Verneinung: *needn't*) ○ *must not:* Verbot ○ *shall:* Vorschlag ○ *should:* Ratschlag ○ *will* (als modales Hilfsverb): Wahrscheinlichkeit	Samuel can swim very well. Lily can watch a DVD tonight while her parents are gone. Murat can't ride a bike because his foot is broken. May I have some chocolate, please? You must listen to your teacher. You must not talk to your neighbour during the exam. Shall we go to Stacey's tonight? You should study for your exam. You're hot. Some water will make you feel better soon.

Üben

5 Modale Hilfsverben

Übung 1

Es gibt im Englischen verschiedene Möglichkeiten, die deutschen Hilfsverben zu übersetzen. Ordne richtig zu.

can – shall – ought to – might – must – to be able to – may – to have to – should – to be allowed to – need	not to have to – mustn't – not to be allowed to – may not – not to be able to – needn't – shouldn't – cannot

können: _____

nicht können: _____

müssen: _____

nicht dürfen: _____

sollen: _____

nicht müssen: _____

dürfen: _____

nicht brauchen: _____

brauchen: _____

nicht sollen: _____

Übung 2

Im Straßenverkehr. Verwende das richtige modale Hilfsverb, um die Straßenschilder und Verkehrssituationen zu erklären.

Children _____ play here.

Drivers _____ be very careful.

Bikers _____ use the bicycle lane.

You _____ smoke here.

You _____ get a ticket if you misbehave in traffic.

Wissen

5 Modale Hilfsverben

5.2 Modale Hilfsverben im **simple past**

Um auch in anderen Zeiten als im Präsens Fähigkeiten, Erlaubnisse, Möglichkeiten, Bitten, Pflichten, Verbote, Vorschläge oder Wahrscheinlichkeiten ausdrücken zu können, haben einige Hilfsverben **Ersatzformen.**	She **was able to** help her little sister with the homework. I **had to** tidy my room. I **was allowed to** stay up until midnight.
Das Hilfsverb *can* bildet das *past tense* entweder mit *could* oder mit dem *simple past* von *to be able to.*	Noah **could ride** a bike when he was four years old. / Noah **was able to ride** a bike when he was four years old.
Merke: Während mit *can / could* ein Können oder etwas Gelerntes ausgedrückt wird, bedeutet *to be able to,* dass jemand fähig ist, etwas zu tun.	At my age my mother **could** swim faster than me. (= sie hatte es gelernt) *Aber:* When she was twelve, she **was able to** break the Junior Record. (= sie war dazu fähig)
Wird *can* verwendet, um eine Erlaubnis bzw. eine Bitte zu formulieren, dann lautet die Ersatzform im *simple past* **to be allowed to.**	I was allowed to watch TV yesterday. (= ich durfte) *Aber:* I could watch TV yesterday. (= ich konnte, z. B. weil es niemand bemerkt hat oder weil der Fernseher wieder funktionierte)
Die Ersatzform für das Modalverb *must* lautet **to have to.** Die Verneinung der Ersatzform erfolgt im *past tense* mit *did + not.*	I must do my homework. ⇨ I had to do my homework. I didn't have to do my homework because I had my arm in a cast *(Gipsverband).*
Um das Modalverb *must not / mustn't* in der Bedeutung *nicht dürfen* in die Vergangenheit zu setzen, ist die Ersatzform **not to be allowed to** notwendig.	The children mustn't watch TV today. ⇨ They were not allowed to watch TV last week.
Das Modalverb *may* wird mithilfe des Ersatzverbs **to be allowed to** in die Vergangenheit gesetzt.	The children may stay up longer tonight. ⇨ They were allowed to stay up longer last night.

Üben

5 Modale Hilfsverben

Übung 3

Höre dir Track 5 an und ergänze den Text mit dem passenden Modalverb.

5   The fog was so dense I _____ see anything.

My husband and I went out last Saturday night and the children _____

_____ watch TV until 10 p.m.

Peter _____ come to the meeting last night because he

_____ babysit his niece.

She _____ go to the cinema with her friends last weekend.

We went to a concert last night. It started at 8 p.m. and we

_____ leave at 7 p.m. to arrive there on time.

Did you see the movie last night? No, I didn't. I _____ visit

my father in hospital.

I _____ go to Peter's party yesterday, I _____

help my mother in the kitchen.

Übung 4

Was müssen die folgenden Personen tun? Setze die richtige Zeit von **to have to** ein: **simple present** oder **simple past**? Achtung: Einmal musst du **couldn't** einsetzen!

Ella is a teacher. She _____ write school reports twice a year.

Sanvi is a doctor. She _____ help people.

My mum used to work at a dry-cleaners *(Reinigung)*. She _____ iron many, many shirts there.

I _____ do my homework yesterday. I _____ babysit my little niece.

Joe is the father of two toddlers *(Kleinkinder)*. Sometimes, he _____ be very patient.

Lily urged her grandfather to read a story to her. Her grandfather

_____ give in *(nachgeben)*, because otherwise

Lily would have been very upset.

Üben

5 Modale Hilfsverben

Übung 5

Setze die folgenden Sätze ins **simple past**. Beachte, dass sich dabei auch die Zeitangaben ändern können (**tonight** ⇨ **last night**)!

I may watch TV tonight.
_____

She must help her grandfather in the garden.
_____

You mustn't eat so much chocolate.
_____

I can finish the book by Monday.
_____

You must not drive a car before your 18th birthday.
_____

I cannot ride a bike.
_____

Übung 6

Fülle die Lücken mit dem passenden modalen Hilfsverb in der richtigen Zeit.

The weather is fine. _____ (sollen) we go swimming?

I _____ (dürfen) go swimming yesterday.

Last week, school was closed due to major construction work. So I _____ _____ (nicht müssen) go to school for five wonderful weekdays!

Look at the sky. It _____ (werden) rain soon.

Mother to her daughter: "It's cold outside. You _____ (müssen) wear a warm jacket."

The grandmother tells her grandchildren: "At your age, I _____ (müssen) work on the fields ten hours a day."

Annie did not study for her maths exam. She _____ (werden) have a bad result.

Ava walked the dog. Therefore she _____ (dürfen) to go to the party.

Wissen

5 Modale Hilfsverben

5.3 Formulieren mit modalen Hilfsverben

Um eine **Erlaubnis** einzuholen, verwendet man im Englischen am besten *may* oder das etwas weniger förmliche *can*.	May I use your pen, please? Mum, can I have the car tonight?
Ein **Rat** oder ein **Hinweis** wird mithilfe von *should* oder *ought to* formuliert.	You should not eat so much chocolate! You ought to buy this dress, you look really beautiful in it!
Um eine **höfliche Frage** oder **Bitte** zu formulieren, eignen sich die modalen Hilfsverben *may, will, shall, could, would, should*.	May I have a cup of coffee, please? Will you inform your parents that I need to meet them soon, please? Could you please tell Yasmin that I called?
Eine **Notwendigkeit** oder **Verpflichtung** lässt sich am besten mit *must* bzw. *to have to / to have got to* ausdrücken.	All exams must be handed in at noon. I have to see a lawyer because of this terrible accident.
Eine **Fähigkeit** bzw. ein **Können** verlangt *can, could* oder die Ersatzform *to be able to*.	Can you swim? At what age were you able to read?
Verbote werden mit *must not / mustn't* formuliert.	You must not be late tonight.
Um eine **Möglichkeit** auszudrücken, eignen sich: ○ *may, might, can* und *could:* Mit ihnen formuliert man Möglichkeiten, bei denen auch Alternativen denkbar sind. ○ Formulierungen mit *should, ought to* und *must:* Sie beinhalten eine relativ hohe Wahrscheinlichkeit. ○ *will:* Damit formuliert man Ereignisse, die mit ziemlicher Sicherheit eintreten werden.	It may be sunny next weekend. It might rain tonight. It could be cold at the beach. My husband should be home from work by six o'clock. She ought to pick up her daughter from school soon. Look at these clouds! It will rain soon. I will call you tomorrow.
Aufgepasst: Manche Hilfsverben können je nach Situation unterschiedliche Bedeutung haben. Achte daher immer auf den Textzusammenhang!	We may buy a new car very soon. (may ⇨ *Möglichkeit*) *Aber:* The children may watch a DVD tonight. (may ⇨ *Erlaubnis*)

Üben

5 Modale Hilfsverben

Übung 7

Sarah kann viel, aber sie kann nicht alles. – Höre dir Track 6 an und kreuze richtig an.

🎧 6

	yes	no
to dance	☐	☐
to swim	☐	☐
to drive a car	☐	☐
to ride a bike	☐	☐
to ride a horse	☐	☐
to play the piano	☐	☐
to bake muffins and cakes	☐	☐
to cook a good meal	☐	☐
to repair her bike	☐	☐
to repair her dad's car	☐	☐

Übung 8

Ergänze in diesem Dialog das richtige modale Hilfsverb.

Luna: "Mum, _____ I help you with the housework?"

Mother: "Oh thank you, darling! We _____ be quicker, then!"

Luna: "Well, Mum – _____ I go to the cinema tonight?

Ethan _____ ask me out."

Mother: "You _____ finish your homework first!"

Luna: "But Mum, it's Friday! I _____ do my homework tomorrow!"

Mother: "Which movie do you want to see?"

Luna: "That new animated movie. It _____ be a lot of fun."

Mother: "Okay then. But you _____ not walk home alone!

Take your mobile phone with you! You _____

call me, so I _____ pick you up there."

Luna: "Thank you so much, Mum! I promise

I _____ do as you've told me!"

Üben

5 Modale Hilfsverben

Wissen⁺

Modale Hilfsverben

Die Ersatzformen werden nicht nur verwendet, um das *past tense* und andere Zeiten zu bilden, sie helfen auch, ein Modalverb im Passiv (↗ Band 8, Kap. 1.4) oder in der indirekten Rede (↗ Band 8, Kap. 2.4) zu verwenden.

I **must feed** the dog six times a day because it is sick.
Passiv: The dog **had to be fed** six times a day when it was sick.
Liz: "Swimming **can** be very tiring."
Indirekte Rede: Liz said that swimming **could** be very tiring.

Mrs Smith hat eine Woche Urlaub in einem Kloster verbracht. Ergänze die passenden modalen Hilfsverben im **past tense.**

Übung 9

Mrs Smith _____ use her mobile phone that week because the monastery *(Kloster)* was located in an area of radio silence *(Funkstille)*.

She _____ eat ice cream, chocolate or any other candy because of special eating rules.

Mrs Smith _____ read a book at night because there was no electricity, either. But she _____ pray *(beten)* five times a day.

On top of everything, she _____ to speak a word on Sunday. She _____ sleep on a thin mattress on the floor.

But Mrs Smith _____ sleep in because there were prayers at 5 a.m. every morning.

However, she _____ concentrate completely on herself!

At the end of the week, Mrs Smith was very weak and _____ walk very well. But she suggested that her husband _____ try such a retreat *(Rückzug)* himself.

Testen

5 Modale Hilfsverben

Klassenarbeit 1   45 Minuten

Aufgabe 1

(*) Benenne die richtige Ersatzform.

can (können) _____

can (dürfen) _____

must (müssen) _____

must not (nicht dürfen) _____

need not (nicht brauchen) _____

Aufgabe 2

(**) Wandle die Sätze um.

simple present	negative sentence	past tense
I can read.		
She must study hard.		
	You mustn't smoke here.	
	I can't drive a truck.	
You may have an ice cream.		

Testen

5 Modale Hilfsverben

Aufgabe 3

(**) Übersetze.

Darf ich heute Abend ins Kino gehen?
_____

Kann ich bitte noch eine Tasse Tee haben?
_____

Kannst du Fahrrad fahren?
_____

Es kann sein, dass es heute noch schneit.
_____

Würdest du mich nächste Woche am Flughafen abholen?
_____

Soll ich mit dem Hund spazieren gehen?
_____

Aufgabe 4

 Sieh dir an, was du und dein Freund oder deine Freundin können, dürfen, sollen oder müssen. Wähle ein passendes modales Hilfsverb und bilde ganze Sätze.

My best friend	You
stays up till 10 p.m. every night	go to bed at 8 p.m.
lives close to school; walk there	take the bus
visits her/his grandparents often, because they live across her/his house	not visit my grandparents often because they live far away
watch TV only one hour per week	watch TV as much as I want to
not do somersaults *(Purzelbäume)* and cartwheels *(Räder)*	do somersaults and cartwheels

_____
_____
_____
_____
_____
_____

Testen

5 Modale Hilfsverben

Aufgabe 5

(***) Formuliere höfliche Fragen.

What do you say if you want to

... offer somebody a cup of coffee?
_____

... borrow somebody's book?
_____

... suggest going to the cinema?
_____

... inform somebody via e-mail the next day?
_____

Klassenarbeit 2   60 Minuten

Aufgabe 6

(*) Verneine die genannten Modalverben.

may ⇨ _____   ought to ⇨ _____

must ⇨ _____   will _____

Aufgabe 7

(**) Übersetze.

Du solltest nicht spät ins Bett gehen.
_____

Es sollte im Frühling warm sein.
_____

Würdest du bitte machen, was ich dir gesagt habe!
_____

Ich muss jetzt gehen.
_____

Darf ich heute Abend ins Kino gehen?
_____

Testen

5 Modale Hilfsverben

Aufgabe 8

Setze **must, needn't** oder **mustn't** in die Lücken ein.

Mother to child: "When the traffic lights are red you _____ walk. You _____ wait until the lights turn green. And as soon as the lights turn green, you _____ walk, but you _____ run."

Daughter to mother: "Mum, you _____ make a sandwich for me as we have a birthday party at school."

Mother to daughter: "Chloe, it's ten to eight. You _____ run to the station or you will miss your bus. You _____ be late for your exam."

Teacher to class: "Mobile phones _____ be turned off during lessons. You _____ write an essay about the school theatre performance. It _____ be finished by next Friday, so you _____ do it today. Today's youngsters _____ write letters to their friends to stay in contact. Instead, they communicate via the internet."

Aufgabe 9

Verneine die folgenden Sätze.

I must do my homework.
_____

My mother is able to work all night long.
_____

You may smoke inside this building.
_____

She had to clean her shoes after walking through the mud.
_____

It might be a good idea to tell lies.
_____

I could buy my own laptop.
_____

Testen

5 Modale Hilfsverben

Aufgabe 10

Ergänze die folgenden Sätze.

I am so sorry to be late, but I _____ (müssen) fix the puncture on my bike before I could leave.

I _____ (nicht können) lend you my vocabulary book. I _____ (müssen) study the vocabulary myself.

You _____ (sollen) tell your teacher that you didn't do your homework.

He _____ (müssen) be nice to me if he wants me to help him.

_____ (dürfen) I go to the cinema tonight, Dad?

You _____ (nicht können) play with your friend today. You've got a ballet lesson at 5 p.m.

He _____ (müssen) run to the supermarket before it closed.

She _____ (müssen) study medicine before she could work as a doctor.

Aufgabe 11

Übersetze.

Sie muss hart arbeiten, um zu gewinnen.
_____

Im Winter sollte es kalt sein.
_____

Ich brauche jetzt noch nicht zu gehen.
_____

Würdest du jetzt bitte ins Bett gehen?
_____

Es wäre keine gute Idee zu lügen.
_____

Könnte ich bitte ein Eis haben?
_____

Wissen

6 Bedingungssätze

6.1 Der Bedingungssatz Typ I

Sätze, die eine Bedingung oder eine Voraussetzung für ein Geschehen, ein Ereignis oder einen Zustand benennen, werden Bedingungssätze genannt. Sie bestehen aus zwei Teilen: ○ einem Nebensatz (*if*-Satz), der die Bedingung nennt und mit *if* (falls, wenn) eingeleitet wird, und ○ einem Hauptsatz, der die Folge(n) beschreibt.	*if*-Satz (Bedingung) **If** mum has a day off, **If** the sun shines,	Hauptsatz (Folge) she'll have enough time to take me shopping. we will get a tan.
Konjunktionen, die einen Bedingungssatz einleiten können, sind: *if, if not, only if, even if, on condition that, provided that, supposing that, unless*	**Even if** it rains, I won't wear my raincoat. **Unless** it rains, the party will take place outside.	
Merke: Steht der *if*-Satz am Anfang, wird er durch ein Komma vom Hauptsatz abgetrennt. Steht der Hauptsatz am Anfang, kommt kein Komma.	**If** you go to the museum tomorrow**,** just give me a quick call. Just give me a quick call **if** you go to the museum tomorrow.	
Je nachdem, ob die im *if*-Satz genannte Bedingung erfüllbar (Typ I), unwahrscheinlich (Typ II) oder nicht erfüllbar (Typ III) ist, gelten für die Verwendung der Zeiten im Englischen verschiedene Regeln.	If it rains, the flowers will get some natural water. (Typ I) If I lived in the USA, I would like to live in California. (Typ II) If you had driven more carefully, you wouldn't have caused an accident. (Typ III)	
Einen Bedingungssatz des Typs I verwendet man, um eine **erfüllbare** oder **wahrscheinliche** Bedingung auszudrücken. Im *if*-Satz steht *simple present,* im **Hauptsatz** steht das *will-future* oder ein modales Hilfsverb + Infinitiv.	*if*-Satz (Bedingung) If it **snows,** If it **snows,**	Hauptsatz (Folge) we **will go** skiing. they **can build** a snowman.

Üben

6 Bedingungssätze

Übung 1

Höre dir Track 7 an und vervollständige die Sätze. Vergiss nicht, ein Komma zu setzen, wo es benötigt wird.

🎧 7

_____ she will buy a cool T-shirt for me.

_____ I won't come.

Her new dress won't fit, _____.

_____ she will be disappointed.

We will go swimming _____.

I will help you _____.

My husband won't water the garden _____.

_____ she will have to stay on at school after the holidays.

_____ she won't be allowed to go shopping with her friend.

_____ our trip will be expensive.

It will be boring _____.

_____ we will have to buy our tickets soon.

Übung 2

In den folgenden Sätzen sind Fehler versteckt. Erkenne sie und verbessere sie, indem du den ganzen Satz neu schreibst.

If you won't know the answer, you can ask me.
_____

That's the boy who sister is going to London for a term.
_____

If you arrive in York, I'll pick you up from the station.
_____

If you wait a minute, I go with you.
_____

88

Üben

6 Bedingungssätze

Übung 3

Im Märchen **Cinderella** (Aschenputtel) stellt die böse Stiefmutter Cinderella eine Menge Bedingungen, bevor sie zum Ball darf. Verbinde die Satzteile zu sinnvollen Sätzen.

Cinderella, you will only go to the King's ball	even if you are terribly tired.
You will wait for us to come home	if you stay at home.
You will not rest	supposing that you don't go to the ball.
You won't see the prince	if you find a dress for you to wear.
You will not dance with the prince	unless all the peas are in this pot.

Wissen+

Das *present progressive* und *present perfect* im *if*-Satz (Typ I)

Merke: Im *if*-Satz kann auch das **present progressive** stehen. Auch hier steht im Hauptsatz entweder das *will-future* oder ein modales Hilfsverb + Infinitiv.

If the reporters **are interviewing** her right now, the whole world **will know** the news very soon.

Die Verwendung des *present progressive* signalisiert, dass das Geschehen, das einen Einfluss auf die Bedingung hat, noch andauert.

If my father is already preparing dinner, I won't be able to ask for some fish and chips.

In Fällen, in denen die Bedingung bereits eingetreten bzw. geschehen ist, steht im *if*-Satz das **present perfect**. Die Zeiten im Hauptsatz ändern sich nicht.

If my parents **have decided** on a new car, **they will** pay cash for it.
If the Millers **haven't planned** their holidays yet, they **won't be able to find** a nice hotel.

Üben

6 Bedingungssätze

Übung 4

Die Stiefmutter geht und hinterlässt Cinderella eine Menge Arbeit. Wandle die Satzteile in **if**-Sätze um, indem du den vorangegangenen Hauptsatz zum **if**-Satz machst.

> count the peas (1) – mop the floor (2) – prepare breakfast for tomorrow (3) – get the beds ready for your sisters and me (4) – feed the cat (5)

Cinderella, if you are finished with the dishes,

_____ (1).

And if you have counted the peas,

_____ (2).

If _____ ,

_____ (3).

If _____ ,

_____ (4).

If _____ ,

_____ (5).

Wissen+

Modale Hilfsverben im *if*-Satz

Im *if*-Satz kann auch ein modales Hilfsverb *(could, should, would)* + Vollverb stehen. Die Zeiten im Hauptsatz sind unverändert.

Solche *if*-Sätze sagen aus, dass man es für wenig wahrscheinlich hält, dass die Bedingungen eintreffen.

If my sister **moves** to New Zealand, her son **will grow** up bilingually. (⇨ Ich rechne damit, dass meine Schwester umzieht und ihr Sohn zweisprachig aufwächst.)
If my sister **should move** to New Zealand, her son **will grow up** bilingually. (⇨ Ich rechne nicht damit, dass …)

Merke: In *if*-Sätzen, die ein *should* haben, kann das *if* wegfallen. Dann ändert sich die Satzstellung: *should* steht **vor** dem Subjekt (Inversion).

If my sister should move to New Zealand, her son will grow up bilingually.
= **Should my sister move** to New Zealand, her son will grow up bilingually.

Üben

6 Bedingungssätze

Übung 5

Vervollständige die Sätze.

If my mum _____ (to do) the shopping now (!),
she _____ (not can / watch) TV.
Phil _____ (should / to see) the doctor if he
_____ still (!) _____ (to feel) sick.
I _____ (to give) you my smartphone if my
parents _____ (should / to buy) me a new one.

Übung 6

Cinderella bekommt Besuch von einer guten Fee. Wandle die Sätze, die sie zu Cinderella sagt, in if-Sätze um.

She wants Cinderella to stop crying so that she can give her a dress. ⇨
"Cinderella, if you stop _____
_____."

She tells Cinderella to find a pumpkin *(Kürbis)* that she can turn into a coach *(Kutsche)*. ⇨ "_____
_____."

The fairy tells her cat that she needs seven mice that can be turned into six horses and a driver *(Kutscher)*. ⇨ "_____
_____."

She advises Cinderella to leave the ball before midnight so that she will arrive home safely. ⇨ "_____
_____."

She wants Cinderella to believe in her magic so that she will be very happy soon. ⇨
"_____
_____."

Wissen

6 Bedingungssätze

6.2 Der Bedingungssatz Typ II

Wenn die im Nebensatz (*if*-Satz) genannte Bedingung unwahrscheinlich ist, steht im *if*-Satz das **simple past**. Im Hauptsatz wird **would / could / might** + **Infinitiv des Vollverbs** verwendet. Diese Sätze heißen Typ II. *Merke:* Für **Ratschläge** wird im *if*-Satz des Typs II anstelle von *was* (simple past von *to be*) die Form *were* (Konjunktiv von *to be*) verwendet. Die Verbformen im Hauptsatz ändern sich dadurch nicht.	*if*-Satz Hauptsatz (Bedingung) (Folge) If we **won** we **would take** our the lottery, kids to the USA. If Milo **passed** he **could use** my his driving test, car. If I **were** you, I would get up immediately.
If und *when* bedeuten beide *wenn*. Sie werden jedoch unterschiedlich gebraucht:	
○ *If* kann man auch mit *falls* übersetzen. Es handelt sich um eine **Bedingung**, die etwas zur Folge hat.	**If** my sister moves to New Zealand, she will take all her furniture with her. – **Wenn / Falls** meine Schwester nach Neuseeland zieht, … (⇨ es ist aber nicht sicher)
○ Bei *when* ist ein **Zeitpunkt** gemeint, zu dem etwas geschehen wird. Anstatt *wenn* kann man auch *sobald* sagen.	**When** my sisters moves to New Zealand, she will take all her furniture with her. – **Wenn / Sobald** meine Schwester nach Neuseeland zieht … (⇨ es ist bereits sicher)
Aufgepasst: Im *if*-Satz Typ II stehen niemals die modalen Hilfsverben *would*, *might* oder *could*.	Even if she ~~would marry~~ **married** a millionaire, she would still work. Unless they ~~would win~~ **won** the lottery, they could not afford to buy a new house.
Ausnahme: Handelt es sich um eine **höfliche Bitte**, kann auch in beiden Teilsätzen *would* stehen.	If you **would give** me your email address, I **would keep** you informed. (Wenn Sie mir Ihre E-Mail-Adresse geben würden, …)
Will man einen Bedingungssatz als Frage formulieren, rückt der Hauptsatz an den Anfang.	Would you move to Los Angeles *(Hauptsatz)* if you worked as an actress? *(if-sentence)*

Üben

6 Bedingungssätze

 Unterstreiche nur die Bedingungssätze, die im **simple past** stehen.

If Liz misses the bus, she will be late for school. If she is late for school, she will have to do some extra homework. Unless her mum called her school, all the teachers would be mad at her. How come? Because Liz missed her bus yesterday and had to do some extra work for today. If she caught the bus, she would be able to copy yesterday's homework from her friend. So what would you do if you were Liz? – Well, if I were Liz, I would hurry!

 Wähle ein passendes Verb aus dem Wortkasten und setze es in der richtigen Form in die Lücke. Aufgepasst: Viermal musst du ein modales Hilfsverb ergänzen!

to be – (not) to water – to build – to go (2x) – to lend – to be disappointed – to help – to win

If I were a millionaire, I _____ myself a castle.
_____ naked to school if somebody paid you a million dollars?
If I _____ the championship, I would be famous soon.
If my sister had more time, she _____ me with the children.
If you didn't have that book, I _____ it to you.
Would you mind if I _____ late for your party?
If I had a headache as often as you, I _____ and see a doctor.
If it rained tonight, I _____ the flowers.
If there was no snow for Christmas, the children _____ _____.

Übung 7

Übung 8

Üben

6 Bedingungssätze

Übung 9

Vervollständige die folgenden Sätze mit einem Bedingungssatz Typ II. Achtung: Aus verneinten Aussagen werden bejahte **if**-Sätze und umgekehrt!

It rains. If it _didn't rain_, we could go by bike.

I have a lot to do today. If I _____ so much to do, we could go out.

I don't understand these questions. If I _____ them, I could help you with your homework.

The world isn't a better place. If the world _____ a better place, there would be no wars.

Sarah enjoys her work. She wouldn't do it if she _____.

Wissen⁺

Das Wort *würde*

Die Übersetzung des deutschen Wortes *würde* führt häufig zu Fehlern.

Merke: Nur im Hauptsatz wird *würde* mit *would* übersetzt!

Wenn ich nach London **ziehen würde**, …
⇨ If I **moved** to London, …
(nicht: If I ~~would move~~ to London, …)
Ich **würde** nach Hause **gehen**, wenn …
⇨ I **would go** home if …

Übung 10

Übersetze die folgenden Sätze ins Englische und achte auf die richtige Übersetzung von **würde**.

Wenn ich mehr lesen würde, wäre ich besser informiert.
_____

Wenn Ella Liam Geld leihen würde, würde er es ihr nicht zurückgeben.
_____

Was würdest du deinem Brieffreund schreiben, wenn du von ihm einen Brief bekommen würdest?
_____

Wir könnten zusammen Hausaufgaben machen, wenn wir uns treffen würden.
_____

Üben

6 Bedingungssätze

Übung 11

Benutze eigene Ideen, um die nachstehenden Sätze zu vervollständigen.

If I study more for my exams, _____.

I would feel angry if _____.

If I didn't go to school tomorrow, _____.

Would you go to a party if _____?

If my parents allow me to, _____.

Would you mind if _____?

Übung 12

Bilde vollständige **if**-Sätze, indem du die passenden Satzteile zusammensetzt und die Sätze dann aufschreibst. Achtung: Typ I oder Typ II?

If you leave now	if we go to America next year.
If I knew the date	if she won the competition.
We'll visit my aunt in Washington	she'll be angry with herself.
If the book wasn't so expensive	you won't miss the bus.
Janet would be very happy	Sika would buy it.
If Chloe does badly in her test next week	I would send Joe a birthday card.

_____

_____

_____

_____

_____

_____

Wissen

6 Bedingungssätze

6.3 Der Bedingungssatz Typ III

Wenn eine Bedingung nicht mehr erfüllt werden kann (sie sich also auf ein vergangenes Ereignis oder Geschehen bezieht), steht das Verb im *if*-Satz im **past perfect**. Im Hauptsatz wird dann **would / could / might + have + past participle** des **Vollverbs** verwendet. Diese Sätze werden Typ III genannt.	*if*-Satz Hauptsatz (Bedingung) (Folge) If I **had read** I **would have known** the travel book, that the museum was closed on Sundays. If we **had had** we **would have** your address, **visited** your new home.
Wie bei Typ I und II können sowohl Haupt- als auch Nebensatz durch das Hinzufügen von *not* verneint werden. *Merke:* Häufig wird anstelle von *had not* auch die **Kurzform** *hadn't* und anstelle von *would not* die Form *wouldn't* verwendet.	If he **had not / hadn't** come by train, he would have been able to bring along all his many suitcases. If he had come by train, he **would not / wouldn't** have been able to bring along his many suitcases. If he **had not / hadn't** come by car, he **would not / wouldn't** have been able to bring along all his suitcases.
Für die Verwendung von Kurzformen gilt außerdem: ○ Im *if*-Satz kann die Kurzform *'d* anstelle von *had* verwendet werden. ○ Im Hauptsatz ersetzt die Kurzform *'d* das Wort *would*.	If **she'd** (= she had) called, my daughter would have told her the whole story. If she'd called, **she'd** (= she would) have told her the whole story.
Werden Bedingungssätze des Typs III als **Frage** formuliert, steht der Hauptsatz zu Beginn des Satzgefüges.	Would you have moved to Los Angeles if you had got a good job offer?
Beim Typ III kann das *if* im Nebensatz auch weggelassen werden. Dann allerdings tauschen Subjekt und Prädikat ihre Stellung im Satz (Inversion).	If **I had met** him earlier in my life, I would have married him. ⇨ **Had I met** him earlier in my life, I would have married him.

Üben

6 Bedingungssätze

Verbinde die Satzteile zu sinnvollen Sätzen.

Übung 13

If they had known you were in hospital,	I could have cleaned my room before she arrived.
If she had called earlier,	they would have visited you.
If I hadn't had the accident,	I wouldn't have bought a new bike.
If I had seen the poster,	I would have gone to the concert.

Wandle die Aussagesätze in **if**-Sätze des Typs III um.
Aufgepasst: Damit der Satz sinnvoll bleibt, müssen bejahte Sätze verneint werden und umgekehrt.

Übung 14

Beispiel: My daughter didn't buy herself a dress yesterday because she hadn't enough money. ⇨ **If she had had enough money, my daughter would have bought herself a dress yesterday.**

My sister broke her leg because she fell down the stairs.

_____

I couldn't read the instructions because they were in Chinese.

_____

We were late for the party because we got stuck in a traffic jam.

_____

My teacher waited for my mum because he wanted to talk to her.

_____

I didn't go to Milo's party because I forgot to buy a present for him.

_____

Üben

6 Bedingungssätze

Übung 15

★★ Bedingungssatz Typ III – vervollständige die Sätze.

If father _____ (to keep) his promise,

I _____ (to fly) to Los Angeles.

Samira _____ (to pass) her exam if she

_____ (to study) harder.

We _____ (not/to drive) the wrong way if dad

_____ (to follow) my directions.

If I _____ (not/to buy) the concert tickets months ago,

we _____ (to stay) at home last night.

Übung 16

★★★ Verwandle die Aussagen in Bedingungssätze.

Buy this book! Read fascinating stories!

Typ I: If you buy this book, you will read fascinating stories.

Typ II: _____

Typ III: _____

Invite Dave the Magician! Make your party a special event!

Typ I: _____

Typ II: _____

Typ III: _____

Don't smoke! Don't get cancer!

Typ I: _____

Typ II: _____

Typ III: _____

Testen

6 Bedingungssätze

Klassenarbeit 1
45 Minuten

Aufgabe 1

Verbinde die Sätze zu sinnvollen Aussagen.

If Lana had sent a SMS,	she could still wear her trendy pair of jeans.
I would have met them at the airport	if you pass your exam.
If Elise wouldn't eat so much chocolate,	her friends would have known where she was.
If you fail your exam,	if they had informed me about their flight number and times.
We will take you to Disneyland	we will stay at home.

Aufgabe 2

Setze die Verben in den Klammern in die richtige Zeit.

If it rains, I _____ (to take) my umbrella.

I _____ (to close) all schools if I were Prime Minister.

Would you be glad if someone _____ (to buy) your old car?

If you don't have an interesting book to read, I _____ (to lend) you one.

We would all still go on horseback if nobody _____ (to invent) the motor engine.

If he had played a bad concert, his mother _____ _____ (to be disappointed).

_____ (to read) more if you had more time?

If it snows tomorrow, we _____ (to build) a snowman.

Your hair _____ (to look) better if you hadn't cut it.

Testen

6 Bedingungssätze

Aufgabe 3

 Unterstreiche die richtige Verbform.

If the sun shines, we will go / would go / can go sailing.

My brother would have passed his driving test if he stopped / had stopped / could have stopped at the red traffic light.

We would not have been informed / could not have been informed / had not be informed if we hadn't had our mobile phone.

Aufgabe 4

 Übersetze.

1. Wenn es morgen regnet, findet unser Ausflug nicht statt.
2. Mein Hund wäre nicht gestorben, wenn er rechtzeitig Medikamente bekommen hätte.
3. Lea würde sich sehr freuen, wenn Max zu ihrer Party kommen würde.
4. Du kannst die Hausaufgaben bei mir abschreiben, wenn du sie nicht hast.
5. Wenn ich Spanisch sprechen könnte, würde ich meine Freundin in Argentinien besuchen.
6. Können wir morgen segeln gehen, falls die Sonne scheint?
7. Wenn ich mehr Taschengeld bekäme, könnte ich viel öfter ins Kino gehen.

Testen

6 Bedingungssätze

Klassenarbeit 2 — 45 Minuten

Aufgabe 5

Es gibt drei unterschiedliche Arten von **if**-Sätzen. Ergänze die Tabelle.

	Art der Bedingung	if-Satz	Hauptsatz	Beispiel
Typ I		if + simple present		If you don't do your homework, you'll get a bad mark.
Typ II		if + simple past		If school finished early, I would go shopping with my friend.
Typ III		if + past perfect		If I had known that she hated fish, I wouldn't have taken her to the Aquarium.

Aufgabe 6

Typ I, II oder III? Bestimme die Bedingungssätze.

If Grandma has got enough eggs in her fridge, she will bake a cake. (____) If she bakes a cake, she will serve it only after lunch. (____) If she serves it after lunch, she will also make some tea. (____) Why will Grandma wait until after lunch? Because she made a cake yesterday, too. Also yesterday, the kids had discovered the cake as soon as they came home from school and had begged to eat a piece of it before lunch. So what? Mary, her daughter, has become very angry with Grandma: If the kids hadn't eaten so much cake before lunch, they would have been hungry enough to finish up their potatoes and vegetables. (____) So what would you do if you were Grandma? (____) I bet you'd hide your cake, too!

Testen

6 Bedingungssätze

Aufgabe 7

Setze das angegebene Verb in die richtige Form. Achte dabei auf die korrekte Verwendung der Zeit.

If you eat more than two pieces of cake, you _____ (to be) ill.

My dad _____ (to earn) more money if he worked more.

The sun might shine tomorrow. Well, if the sun _____ (to shine) tomorrow, I _____ (to go) swimming.

Samuel _____ (not/to fall) from his bike if he _____ (to look) more closely at the road.

What are you doing? – I am writing a love letter. – What will you do if you _____ (to finish) it? – If I _____ (to finish) the letter, I _____ (to send) it to my boyfriend, of course!

Aufgabe 8

Ergänze die Sätze. Richte dich dabei nach den Angaben, die am Satzende in Klammern stehen.

Harper _____ to the theatre tonight if she _____ time. (Typ I, to go, to have)

If my wife _____ so much money, I guess I _____ to work full-time. (Typ II, not/to have, to have)

If I _____ the lottery, I _____ a round-the-world-ticket and see the world. (Typ II, to win, to buy)

I _____ from the airport if you _____ me an e-mail with your flight number and arrival time. (Typ I, to pick up, to send)

If we _____ your address, we _____ you a postcard from Las Vegas. (Typ III, to have, to send)

Testen

6 Bedingungssätze

 Aufgabe 9

Übersetze.

Wenn der Rettungswagen schneller da gewesen wäre, hätte sie überlebt.

_____

Wenn ich nach London umziehen würde, könnte ich nur in einer kleinen Wohnung leben.

_____

Falls ich Großvater besuche, grüße ich ihn von dir.

_____

Falls meine Schwester nach Neuseeland umzieht, nimmt sie all ihre Möbel mit.

_____

Klassenarbeit 3 45 Minuten

 Aufgabe 10

Suche dir aus dem Wortkasten die jeweils richtige zweite Satzhälfte.

> it had not rained – she met a very rich, attractive young man –
> you put them into the fridge –
> their pupils forget to do their homework –
> I wanted to lose some pounds

All fruit except bananas stay fresh if …

_____

Most teachers get angry if …

_____

Hannah would marry Tom right away even if …

_____

I would eat less chocolate if …

_____

We would have gone on a long bike ride if …

_____

Testen

6 Bedingungssätze

Aufgabe 11 Unterstreiche die richtige Verbform.

If it is sunny, we must go / will go / can go biking.

You could earn more money some day if you studied / had studied / would have studied harder in school.

I had rented / would have rented / would rent that flat if I had understood the landlady correctly.

We won't be able to buy a brand new car if your mother doesn't pay / won't pay / isn't going to pay for it.

If I don't go to Phil's party, he won't be / had been / would have been too disappointed.

If it had been sunny, it will be / could be / would have been much warmer.

Aufgabe 12 Ergänze die folgenden Sätze.

If my daughter saves enough money, she _____ (can / to buy) her own car as soon as she turns eighteen.

If Maggie had practised enough for her driving test, she _____ (to pass) the exam.

If I _____ (to be) a dog, I would like to live with my family.

If you travel to the USA, you _____ (must / to have) a passport.

If I had known that she is allergic to milk, I _____ (not / to offer) her that cheesecake.

The Millers _____ (to enjoy) their Californian holidays if they hadn't had a bad accident.

Sarah _____ (to lose) money if she goes into that casino.

The trip _____ (to be) cheaper if you could stay for ten days instead of two weeks.

If I were you, I _____ (to try) eat more healthily.

Testen

6 Bedingungssätze

Aufgabe 13

Was wäre, wenn ...? Formuliere sinnvolle Antwortsätze.

What would you do if your boyfriend/girlfriend kissed someone else?
<u>If my boyfriend/girlfriend kissed someone else, I</u>
_____

What would you do if you smelled smoke from a fire?
_____
_____

What would you do if you weren't prepared for your maths exam?
_____
_____

What would you do if you found a spider in your bag?
_____
_____

What would you do if you met your favourite youtube star?
_____
_____

Aufgabe 14

Höre dir Track 8 an und ergänze die folgenden Sätze.

8

If Jan lived in England, _____.
Jan would be late for school _____.
He will cycle to school today _____.
If he waits, _____.
If the summer is warm and sunny, Jan and his friends _____
_____
But they must go by bus _____.

Wissen

7 Nebensätze und Ergänzungen

7.1 Adverbialsätze

Adverbialsätze *(adverbial clauses)* sind durch einleitende **Konjunktionen** mit dem Hauptsatz verbunden.	Grandma often falls asleep **while** she is watching TV.
Ein Adverbialsatz kann **vor oder nach dem Hauptsatz** stehen. Steht er davor, dann wird gewöhnlich ein Komma benutzt.	**When** I entered the living room, Grandma was already sleeping.
Adverbialsätze der Zeit *(adverbial clauses of time)* (↗ Temporalsätze Kap. 7.3):	
after (nachdem), *once* (einmal, einst), *when* (wenn, als), *as* (als), *as soon as* (sobald), *till / until* (bis), *before* (bevor), *since* (seit, seitdem), *while* (während, solange)	I'll phone you **as soon as / when** I arrive in York. You're not going out **until** you have finished this.
Adverbialsätze des Ortes *(adverbial clauses of place)*:	
where (wo), *everywhere* (überall),	Please leave the books **where** you found them.
wherever (wohin auch immer)	**Wherever / Everywhere** she goes, there are people waiting to see her.
Adverbialsätze des Grundes *(adverbial clauses of reason)*:	
because, *since* (weil), *as* (da)	We are leaving **because** we are tired. **As** she grew older, she changed a lot.
Adverbialsätze der Einräumung / des Gegensatzes *(adverbial clauses of contrast)*:	
while (während), *even if*, *even though* (auch wenn, obwohl), *although / though* (obwohl / obgleich)	**Although / Even if** it was already quite late, Kim was still working on her essay.
Adverbialsätze des Zwecks / der Folge *(adverbial clauses of purpose)*:	
so / so that (sodass, damit)	I have so many DVDs **so that** I don't know where to put them.
Adverbialsätze des Vergleichs *(adverbial sentences of comparison)*:	
as (wie, so wie), *as if / as though* (als ob)	The cat is sitting in front of the radio **as if** it is listening to the programme.

Üben

7 Nebensätze und Ergänzungen

Übung 1

Verbinde die Satzteile zu sinnvollen Sätzen.

They went on	as soon as you can.
They were playing tennis	because the holiday was over.
They turned back	until they came to a small farm.
Mr Campbell warned them about the dangers	before they left.
Get back	although it started to rain.
I felt really sorry	when the weather changed.

Übung 2

Entscheide dich für die richtige Konjunktion und unterstreiche sie.

The tour guide always warns the tourists before / because they leave.

Our neighbours went out because / although the weather was bad.

Give me your phone number so that / before I can phone you.

You should wait before / until the weather forecast is really good.

Übung 3

Vervollständige die folgenden Sätze mithilfe einer passenden Konjunktion und den angegebenen Satzbausteinen.

while – where – as if – wherever

she was sitting – the place – they are paying attention – I go

The beach is _____ I most like to be in the summer.

It is terribly loud in this house _____ .

There was a huge bird above her _____ in the garden.

The students are sitting behind their desks _____ _____ to their teacher.

Üben

7 Nebensätze und Ergänzungen

Übung 4

Höre dir Track 9 an und setze die passende Konjunktion ein.

9

Please call me _____ you know the result.

I haven't seen her _____ we had an argument two weeks ago.

_____ you go, always take some money along!

For their anniversary *(Hochzeitstag)*, they went back to the place _____ they first met.

I didn't like the movie _____ it was very bloody.

_____ I have no money, I will stay at home this summer.

_____ I don't like jazz music, I didn't complain about the party at our neighbours.

_____ the time she gets home, dinner will be cold again.

I sent the letter by express mail _____ it would arrive the next day for sure.

Wissen+

Adverbialsätze des Grundes

Because wird eher in nachgestellten Adverbialsätzen verwendet, mit *as* und *since* eingeleitete Adverbialsätze werden gewöhnlich vorangestellt.

As it is so cold today, I'll wear trousers.
Since Katie has no money, she can't buy the ticket.
I have to work hard because I'm going to take an exam soon.

Üben

7 Nebensätze und Ergänzungen

Übung 5

10

Höre dir Track 10 zweimal an und beantworte die Fragen. Verwende bei der Beantwortung der Fragen die Konjunktionen aus dem Kasten.

although – until – because – if – then

Why is Kim a naughty girl?
_____

What is a pity?
_____

Kim watched a programme about animals. What did she do next?
_____

How long did she play cards with her parents?
_____

What will Kim do next weekend?
_____

Übung 6

Benutze jeweils eine der folgenden Konjunktionen und vervollständige die Sätze über deine letzten Ferien.

I really enjoyed the holiday …
_____

I felt at home …
_____

I'd like to try a holiday in the USA next year …
_____

We had a lot of fun …
_____

It was a fantastic holiday …
_____

Üben

7 Nebensätze und Ergänzungen

Wissen+

Adverbien der Art und Weise (adverbs of manner) wie: *terribly, happily, well, fast* beschreiben, wie jemand etwas tut oder wie etwas geschieht. Meistens werden sie gebildet, indem einfach **–ly** an das Adjektiv angehängt wird. Sie stehen meist nach dem direkten Objekt. Wenn keins vorhanden ist, nach dem Verb.	I miss my boyfriend terribly. They lived happily ever after. If you don't feel well, stay at home!
Achtung: Im Deutschen haben Adjektive und Adverbien der Art und Weise dieselbe Form. Im Englisch nicht.	My mother's French is very good. She can speak French very well.
Adverbien des Grades (adverbs of degree) wie *totally, really, quite, a bit* verstärken oder schwächen andere Wörter ab, vor denen sie stehen.	I totally agree with you. She quite likes him.
Merke: Treffen Adverbien der Art und Weise, des Ortes und der Zeit aufeinander, gilt *manner – place – time*	My brother secretly married his girlfriend in Manchester last Friday.

 Adjektiv oder Adverb? Füge das passende Wort ein.

Übung 7

thankful – badly – proudly – used – well – desperate – hard – new – terrible

Our car doesn't work anymore. I wrongly said that it must have been my sister's _____ driving style. My father was _____ because he _____ needs a car. Life can be very _____! I can search the internet very _____. So my father asked me to look for a cheap _____ car on the internet. That's how I found out that there is a _____ car sharing company in the area with reasonable prices. I _____ showed my father the offer. He was extremely _____.

110

7 Nebensätze und Ergänzungen

7.2 Objektergänzungen

Notwendige Objektergänzung

Bei bestimmten Verben steht **nach dem direkten Objekt** noch eine notwendige Ergänzung zu diesem Objekt *(object complement)*.

Diese Ergänzung kann ein **Substantiv** oder ein **Adjektiv** sein.

They call this place Piano Bar. (⇨ die Ergänzung "Piano Bar" ist ein Substantiv)
He found life very hard. (⇨ die Ergänzung "hard" ist ein Adjektiv)

Nach folgenden Verben steht nach dem direkten Objekt eine notwendige Ergänzung:

to call – nennen	My name is George. But my wife calls me Georgie.
to crown – krönen zu	When was Henry VIII crowned king?
to declare – erklären zu	This area was declared a national park in 1998.
to find – finden, halten für	We didn't find the film boring.
to make – machen	The test results made our English teacher very angry.
to think – halten für	My parents think sports useful.

Daraus ergibt sich folgende Satzstellung:
Subjekt + Verb + Objekt + Ergänzung

Objektergänzung mit as

Aufgepasst: Bei manchen Verben wird die Objektergänzung mit der Präposition *as* angeschlossen:

to choose as – wählen zu	The company chose Mrs Smith as a chairwoman.
to describe as – beschreiben als	My mum often describes me as a very lazy boy.
to treat as – behandeln wie	Some teachers treat us as criminals.

Üben

7 Nebensätze und Ergänzungen

Übung 8

⭐ Wie kannst du etwas nennen? Benutze die Adjektive aus dem vorangegangenen Satz und verwende **to call**.

The hotel is wonderful. – Really? I don't _____.

What a lovely meal! – How can you _____ ?

This man is miserable. – Oh no! You can't _____.

Übung 9

⭐⭐ Wähle jeweils ein Adjektiv oder ein Substantiv aus dem Wortkasten und ergänze damit die folgenden Sätze.

> necessary – difficult – an idiot – nervous –
> king – as a close friend

This exam makes me _____.

Who crowned him _____ ?

The class found these exercises _____.

Stop calling me _____.

All my teachers think homework _____.

Can you describe Marc _____ ?

Übung 10

⭐⭐⭐ Ergänze die Sätze mit deinen eigenen Ideen.

People in Great Britain are friendly. They make you feel _____.

Have you ever been to Wales? You call the people there _____.

People in Scotland wear skirts. You call those skirts _____.

You should visit London and its sights. You'll find them _____.

Have you ever tried baked beans? Some people think them _____.

Those buses in London are world-famous. People call them _____.

I hope you have good weather. Good weather always makes a holiday _____.

Wissen

7 Nebensätze und Ergänzungen

7.3 Temporalsätze

Temporalsätze oder Adverbialsätze der Zeit *(clauses of time)* geben an, **wann** etwas geschieht.

Temporalsätze werden mit verschiedenen **Konjunktionen** eingeleitet. Zu ihnen gehören:

as soon as – sobald	Kim will phone her parents as soon as she arrives in New York.
as – als, während	She was watching him as he was getting ready.
till / until – bis	You are not going out until you have finished this.
before – bevor	Lock the doors before you leave.
when – als, wenn	When we arrived, the whole family welcomed us.
since – seit	What have you been doing since we last met?
while – während	While I was waiting at the bus stop, it started to rain.

Aufgepasst: **If** und **when** können beide mit *wenn* übersetzt werden, haben aber dennoch unterschiedliche Bedeutung:
- *If* leitet einen Bedingungssatz (= falls) ein,
- *when* (= sobald) einen Temporalsatz.

If I'm late this evening, don't wait for me.

When I get home this evening, I'm going to have a shower.

Der Unterschied zwischen **as** und **when**:
- *As* wird benutzt, wenn zwei Dinge zur gleichen Zeit passieren,
- *when* wird benutzt, wenn eins nach dem anderen passiert.

As I walked into the room, the phone started ringing.
When I got home, I had a bath.

In Temporalsätzen wird auch dann, wenn über ein zukünftiges Ereignis gesprochen wird, nicht die Zukunftsform des Verbs benutzt. Die **Zukunft** wird nur im **Hauptsatz** verwendet, während im **Nebensatz** das *present tense* steht.

We will stay here until you get back.
The children won't be at home when we arrive.

Üben

7 Nebensätze und Ergänzungen

Übung 11

Verwende die Konjunktionen aus dem Wortkasten, um die Sätze zu vervollständigen.

since – as soon as – before – until – while

I'll go to the United States _____ I'm 18.

It began to rain _____ Mr Lennox was working in the garden.

Don't forget your coat _____ you go outside.

Josh will stay here _____ you come back.

The pupils have been quiet _____ the teacher entered the room.

Übung 12

If oder **when**? – Entscheide dich für die richtige Konjunktion.

_____ I'm late tonight, don't wait for me.

I'm going to town. _____ I come back, we can have our tea.

Do you mind _____ I smoke in here?

_____ Tony uses his bike, he always wears his helmet.

Übung 13

Hier musst du dich zwischen **as** und **when** entscheiden. Verbinde die Satzteile mit Linien und wähle die richtige Konjunktion.

We were all waving goodbye	as	I was cycling along the street.
Eve smiled	when	I was preparing the vegetables.
I cut myself	as	Hugh drove away in his car.
A dog ran out in front of my bike	when	her father took a photo of her.

114

Üben

7 Nebensätze und Ergänzungen

 Bilde aus zwei Sätzen einen: Verbinde die beiden Hauptsätze zu einem Hauptsatz mit Temporalsatz + Konjunktion.

Übung 14

We'll arrive back home tomorrow. Then I'll phone Sarah.
 When we arrive back home tomorrow, I will phone Sarah.

Pat was drawing some pictures. There was some noise outside.
_____

George must wait at home. Then his mum comes back.
_____

First Marvin should eat something. Then he can go out with Kenyi.
_____

Mrs Patel sat down. At the same time the phone rang.
_____

The pupils are standing at the bus stop. The bus hasn't arrived yet.
_____

Jenna lives in Howard Road. She moved there last year.
_____

 Vervollständige die Sätze mithilfe der Verben im Wortkasten. Benutze die richtige Konjunktion und achte auf die richtige Zeit.

Übung 15

> to finish your homework – ~~to cross the road~~ – to come back – to have a shower – to be away on holiday

Timmy, you must always look both ways before you cross the road .

Our neighbour will feed our cats _____.

I'm going to bed _____.

The Watsons will visit us _____.

I'll wait for you _____.

Testen

7 Nebensätze und Ergänzungen

Klassenarbeit 1  30 Minuten

Aufgabe 1 Bilde vollständige Sätze, indem du die passenden Satzteile mit Linien verbindest. Achte darauf, dass du die richtige Konjunktion wählst.

We didn't get wet	wherever	the actors played their parts badly.
My dog is sitting behind the door	as if	the princess kissed it.
The film was terrible	when	we had fastened our seat belts.
It was foggy	as soon as	my father drove into London.
My friend always stops	although	to be waiting for me.
The plane took off	because	she sees a shoe shop.
My father bought a paper	after	it was raining.
The frog turned into a prince	so that	he could read the latest news.

Aufgabe 2 Bilde Adverbialsätze mit den folgenden Satzteilen. Benutze die passenden Konjunktionen und achte auf die richtige Zeit.

Yesterday / Yasmin / to slip / to get off the bus

_____

The Robinsons / to have / their pond / they moved house

_____

Mr Smith / to hate / loud music / it / to give him / a headache

_____

Last night / Tom and Kate / to go / cinema / they / to be tired

_____

My father / often / to eat / sweets / to work / on his computer

_____

Testen

7 Nebensätze und Ergänzungen

Aufgabe 3

Übersetze die folgenden Adverbialsätze ins Englische.

Wenn du rennst, dann wirst du den Bus noch bekommen.
___

Obwohl Jamila sehr müde war, konnte sie nicht schlafen.
___

Sobald Herr Miller nach Hause kommt, schaltet er das Radio an.
___

Jack verließ die Party früher, weil er Kopfschmerzen hatte.
___

Wo wirst du übernachten, wenn du in London bist?
___

Während Lilly am Strand war, las sie viel.
___

Klassenarbeit 2

 45 Minuten

Aufgabe 4

Welche Konjunktion passt nicht in die Reihe? Streiche sie durch.

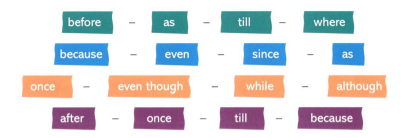

Testen

7 Nebensätze und Ergänzungen

Aufgabe 5

Ergänze den zweiten Teil des Objekts mit den Ausdrücken aus dem Wortkasten.

feel welcome – Sue – lochs – crazy – strange – pleasant

There are lot of lakes in Scotland. There you call them _____.

Sunshine and high temperatures always make a holiday _____.

People in Ireland are friendly. They will always make you _____.

Have you heard about Sarah's plans? – Yes, but I find her idea _____.

Most people in our town find our neighbour a bit _____.

Her name is Susan. But I'm sure you can call her _____.

Aufgabe 6

Setze die passende Konjunktion ein und bestimme, um welche Art von Nebensatz es sich handelt.

as soon as – because – as if – after – which – before

They enjoyed a candlelight dinner _____ it had gotten dark.

Art des Nebensatzes: _____

I lost my purse _____ I had bought in New York.

Art des Nebensatzes: _____

You can go out _____ you have finished your homework.

Art des Nebensatzes: _____

He looked at me _____ he knew me.

Art des Nebensatzes: _____

It had started to rain _____ the party had begun.

Art des Nebensatzes: _____

She was worried _____ they were late for their appointment.

Art des Nebensatzes: _____

Testen

7 Nebensätze und Ergänzungen

Aufgabe 7

Übersetze die folgenden Sätze und achte auf die richtige Übersetzung der Objektergänzungen.

Schotten sollten nicht Engländer genannt werden.
_____

Die meisten Eltern denken, dass Obst und Gemüse gesund sind.
_____

Ich würde ihn als einen netten Jungen beschreiben.
_____

Die Schüler finden das Buch spannend.
_____

Behandele mich nicht wie ein Kind!
_____

Aufgabe 8

Formuliere ganze Sätze aus den durcheinandergewürfelten Satzfetzen. Achte dabei auf die richtige Reihenfolge der Adverbien.

On the phone – for dinner next Sunday – asked us – the waiter – politely – if we wanted – in the garden – to sit
_____
_____

next August – She – to Canada with her cousin – agreed to go on holiday – because she loves nature – happily
_____
_____

at midnight – our father – secretly – to a party – went
_____

ran into his car – drove to Dover – carefully – but a cow – he – last night
_____

Wissen

8 Englisch lernen

8.1 Thematischer Lernwortschatz

Der Wortschatz im Englischen lässt sich in einen Grundwortschatz und einen Aufbauwortschatz aufteilen.

Der **Grundwortschatz** beinhaltet die häufigsten Wörter, Wortverbindungen und Redewendungen. Mit ihm kannst du Gespräche auf Englisch führen oder auch schon Briefe / Mails etc. an englischsprachige Freundinnen und Freunde schreiben.	**transport and travelling:** bus, plane, underground, ferry, to go by, to walk, to fly, to land, to drive, to sail
Der **Aufbauwortschatz** baut auf den Grundwortschatz auf und erweitert diesen. Er hilft dir, dich zu einem bestimmten Sachverhalt mit einem breit gefächerten Vokabular zu äußern.	**transport and travelling:** coach *(Reisebus)*, underground network *(U-Bahnnetz)*, destination *(Reiseziel)*, dining car *(Speisewagen)*, sleepers *(Schlafwagen)*, to depart *(abfahren)*, on schedule *(pünktlich)*

Im Unterricht lernst du Vokabeln meist in einem inhaltlichen Zusammenhang: Jede Lektion ist einem **Themenschwerpunkt** zugeordnet. Daher ist es sinnvoll, Vokabeln auch nach Themen zu lernen. Hilfreich sind **Wortfelder, Bilder** oder **Diagramme** *(mind maps)*.

Themenschwerpunkt "school": primary school *(Grundschule)*, secondary school *(weiterführende Schule)*, comprehensive school *(Gesamtschule)*, boarding school *(Internat)*, school report *(Zeugnis)*

Weitere **Tipps zum Vokabellernen:**
○ Lerne in **kleinen Lernportionen:** höchstens 20 Vokabeln pro Tag, am besten in Zehnerblöcke aufgeteilt.
○ Lege eine **Lernkartei** an: Sortiere Wörter, die du zweimal gewusst hast, aus und konzentriere dich auf die Vokabeln, die du nicht beherrschst.
○ Schreibe besonders schwierige Vokabeln auf gut sichtbar aufgehängte **Lernplakate** oder **-poster.**
○ Sprich (nicht mehr als zehn) Vokabeln auf ein Gerät, mit dem du aufnehmen kannst: mit Pausen zum Nachsprechen oder Übersetzen.

Wortfeld "temperature": hot, warm, cool, cold;
"travelling": ticket, passport, suitcase

Diagramm (mind map) "clothes":

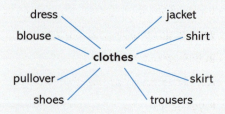

Üben

8 Englisch lernen

Übung 1

* In der Stadt – was ist auf den folgenden Bildern dargestellt?

_____   _____

_____   _____

Übung 2

** Finde das Gegenteil zu den folgenden Begriffen.

town ⇔ _____   boring ⇔ _____

quiet ⇔ _____   stressful ⇔ _____

Übung 3

** Vervollständige den folgenden Text mit den richtigen Ausdrücken.

London is an _____ city. There are theatres and cinemas, so there's _____ to see. Let's _____ a bus to go to the museum. Every year many tourists go _____ in London. If we want to go shopping, we must go _____. Some people don't live in the city but in the _____.

A lot of farmers use their fields to _____ potatoes and vegetables. If you spend your holidays on a farm you can enjoy the animals there such as _____ and _____.

Üben

8 Englisch lernen

Übung 4

Verbinde die Adjektive mit passenden Substantiven.

rich	factory
flat	farmland
large	museum
wild	area
ugly	forest
hilly	landscape
fascinating	city
crowded	rock

Übung 5

Benutze nun die Ausdrücke aus der Übung 4 und schreibe die Dinge auf, die du positiv und negativ am Stadtleben oder Landleben findest. Formuliere sechs Sätze und begründe deine Antworten. Die Ausdrücke im Wortkasten können dir dabei behilflich sein.

> I like / don't like … – I hate … – I can't stand … –
> I enjoy … – … is / are terrible because …
> I think … is / are OK – I think … is good / terrible / …

_____
_____
_____
_____

Übung 6

Beschreibe in vier bis sechs Sätzen die Gegend, in der du wohnst. Benutze weitgehend Vokabeln aus diesem Kapitel.

_____
_____
_____
_____

Wissen

8 Englisch lernen

8.2 Text- und Hörverständnis

Lesen und Verstehen

Zunächst fragt man nach der **Textsorte:** Handelt es sich z. B. um eine Geschichte, einen Bericht, einen Brief, ein Drama, Gedicht oder eine Informationsbroschüre?

What kind of text is it? ⇨ The text is a story / report / letter / play / poem …

Der nächste Schritt ist die Frage nach dem **Thema des Textes.** Dabei können die Überschrift, der Einleitungssatz oder das Bildmaterial von großer Hilfe sein.

What is the text about? ⇨ The story / report is about …, It has / gives important facts / information about …

When you read the headline / first passage you expect to read about …

Beim Lesen sollte man den Text sowohl in seiner Gesamtheit als auch seine Details erfassen können.

- Zum **Gesamtverständnis** *(reading for gist)* helfen Überschrift, Schlüsselwörter *(keywords)*, Bilder oder der erste Textabschnitt.

The Romans in Europe; The Roman Empire

- Zum **Detailverständnis** *(reading for detail)* liest man den Text ein zweites Mal, unterstreicht die Schlüsselwörter und macht sich zu ihnen **Notizen.**

"Roman baths":
– daily life
– important role for the hygiene
– social function

- **Unbekannte Wörter** können auf folgende Weise erschlossen werden:
- Sind Wörter aus derselben Wortfamilie (Nomen, Verb, Adjektiv …) bekannt?

friendship – friend – friendly – unfriendly

- Sind Wörter aus demselben Wortfeld bekannt?

school: pupil, teacher, desk, pencil, chalk, to write in an exercise book, break, cafeteria, to have detention

- Sind dir gleich- oder ähnlich lautende Wörter aus einer anderen Sprache (Deutsch, Latein, Französisch etc.) bekannt?

saxophone: Saxophon (D), saxophone (F)
parents : parentes (L)

- In welchem Kontext steht das Wort?

The Roman baths had "changing rooms". ⇨ A changing room has got something to do with "to change" and the context is about a bath. ⇨ *Umkleidekabine*

- Werden in den Aufgaben Synonyme von Wörtern im Gelesenen verwendet?

to enjoy / to like very much

Wissen

8 Englisch lernen

Hörverstehen

Lies die Aufgabenstellungen sorgfältig und unterstreiche Schlüsselbegriffe. Finde heraus, welche Art von Antwort du jeweils geben musst (Lücken füllen, ankreuzen, selbst formulieren etc.).
Stelle dich mental auf die Art des Textes ein (Thema, Gesprächssituation etc.).

Erstes Hören:

Gehe genau so vor wie beim Leseverstehen: achte auf verwandte Formulierungen zu den Schlüsselbegriffen in der Aufgabenstellung (hörst du Wörter aus der gleichen Wortfamilie, dem gleichen Wortfeld, Synonyme?).
Markiere dir die Stellen, wo du nach dem ersten Hören noch unsicher bist bei der Beantwortung.

Zweites Hören:

Achte nun insbesondere auf die Stellen, wo du dir hinsichtlich der Antwort noch nicht sicher warst.

Achtung: Häufiger sind in der Aufgabenstellung sogenannte Distraktoren enthalten. Dies kommt oft bei Ankreuzübungen vor, wenn die Antwortmöglichkeiten extra so gewählt wurden, um dich auf eine falsche Fährte zu locken.

Max: "You know what? I have seen a lot of jewels last week. My aunt is very rich and showed me around her house."
What happened while Max was at his aunt's?
a) He saw jewels. ✓
b) He saw Jules.
c) He saw his aunt's apartment.
explanation: similar pronunciation of jewels and Jules.

Merke: In der Regel werden die Fragen in chronologischer Reihenfolge zum Gehörten gestellt.
Sprachliche Fehler bei der Beantwortung von Hörverstehensaufgaben werden in der Schule immer nur gewertet, wenn sie das Verständnis beeinträchtigen.
Im Unterricht und in der Arbeit wirst du Hörverstehenstexte immer zweimal hören.

Üben

8 Englisch lernen

Beschreibe anhand des Bildes und der Überschrift auf Englisch, wovon der darauf folgende Text handeln könnte. Begründe deine Antwort.

Übung 7

Sarah's first holiday alone

_____
_____
_____
_____

Lies nun den dazugehörigen Text aufmerksam durch.

Übung 8

When the train arrived, it was almost empty. Sarah Hill had already been standing on platform 9 at King's Cross Station in London for about ten minutes. It was a sunny day, almost cloudless. Sarah had just said good-bye to her father.
She was on her way to Yorkshire to visit her mother who worked there as a vet.

Sarah lived with her father in London, the city of cities. She loved London, so she had decided to stay here with her father instead of moving up North when her parents had separated.

Sarah's father didn't like the wild countryside. He always said life in a big city was the only true life. That was one reason for her parents' separation: Mum didn't like big cities because they are dirty, smelly and noisy. She was fond of animals, and she loved her job.

And now Sarah would spend two weeks in Yorkshire. Her mum would meet her in York. She had already told Sarah on the phone about the beautiful landscape, sheep farms, endless fields and the soft green hills.

Sarah got on the train. She was excited: It was her first visit after her parents had split up two years ago, and it was her first holiday without her father. Mr Hill had bought the train tickets, had given her some pocket money and had helped her with the bags. Her father was great – simply helpful and understanding; sometimes strict but never really angry with Sarah.

The train started, and while Sarah, who had her own compartment, was paging through "Mizz Seventeen", her favourite teen mag, the suburbs of London passed by. What if she liked Yorkshire and didn't want to come back …?

Üben

8 Englisch lernen

Übung 9

⚹⚹ Um welche Textsorte handelt es sich bei dem vorliegenden Text? Was erwartest du weiterhin von einem solchen Text? Formuliere zwei Sätze auf Englisch.

_____
_____

Übung 10

⚹⚹ Unterstreiche die unbekannten Wörter im Text, schreibe sie heraus und versuche sie aus dem Zusammenhang zu erklären.

_____
_____
_____
_____
_____
_____

Übung 11

⚹⚹ Beantworte die folgenden Fragen. Lies sie vorher gründlich durch und unterstreiche dann im Text die jeweiligen Textstellen. Beantworte die Fragen in vollständigen Sätzen.

1. What is the weather like?
   _____

2. Where does Sarah want to go? Why?
   _____

3. Why is Sarah excited?
   _____

4. Where will she meet her mother?
   _____

5. What do we learn about Sarah's mother?
   _____

6. Why does Sarah like her father?
   _____

Üben

8 Englisch lernen

Übung 12

Beantworte die folgenden Fragen in vollständigen Sätzen.

1. How would you describe Sarah?

2. Why do you think Sarah hasn't visited her mother so far?

3. Do you think Sarah will come back to London?

4. Living in London or your hometown – what would you like more? Why?

11

Übung 13

Höre dir auf Track 11 den Text über die Geschichte des Tower of London zweimal an und beantworte die Fragen in vollständigen Sätzen. Schreibe in dein Übungsheft.

1. Who began building the Tower of London?

2. What is the White Tower?

3. What could you find there during the Middle Ages?

4. Why are six to seven ravens still there today?

5. How many tourists come every year to visit the Tower of London?

6. Who looks after the Tower of London today?

7. Why are they called Beefeaters?

Üben

8 Englisch lernen

Übung 14

Höre dir auf Track 12 den folgenden Text über Katies Reise zweimal an. Entscheide dann, welche Aussagen wahr und welche falsch sind.

	true	false
12 Katie is on a train from London to Aberdeen.	☐	☐
Katie's grandparents will collect her at the station in Aberdeen.	☐	☐
She is travelling with her parents.	☐	☐
She overslept so she couldn't have a proper breakfast.	☐	☐
She is looking for seat 52.	☐	☐
Katie is travelling at the beginning of the Christmas holidays.	☐	☐
There is an old man sitting next to her.	☐	☐
The man helps her with her luggage.	☐	☐
Katie thinks that the old man is probably old-fashioned and boring.	☐	☐
She starts to listen to some music by a group called 'Milk and Honey'.	☐	☐

Übung 15

Korrigiere die falschen Aussagen aus Übung 14 und schreibe sie korrekt auf. Höre dir, falls nötig, Track 12 nochmals an.

_____
_____
_____
_____
_____
_____
_____
_____

Üben

8 Englisch lernen

Übung 16 (*)

Höre dir Track 13 an und kreuze an, was du gehört hast.

- [ ] a monologue
- [ ] a dialogue
- [ ] a report
- [ ] a play
- [ ] a speech
- [ ] a weather forecast

Übung 17 (**)

Worum geht es im Gehörten? Notiere Schlüsselwörter (keywords).

_____
_____
_____
_____

Übung 18 (**)

Höre dir den Track ein zweites Mal an und beantworte die W-Fragen.

Who? _____
Where? _____
What? _____
When? _____
Why? _____

Übung 19 (***)

Welche Zusammenfassung ist richtig? 1, 2 oder 3?

1. Emma and Jack meet on a plane and talk about a youth forum Jake is interested in.
2. A girl from his school interviews Jack for the school magazine because he wants to solve environmental problems.
3. Sack tells a professional reporter about his involvement in projects to save the planet.

_____

Wissen

8 Englisch lernen

8.3 Wörterbucharbeit

Das Wörterbuch als Arbeitsmittel

Für die Arbeit mit englischen Texten solltest du dir ein mittelgroßes **zweisprachiges Wörterbuch** anschaffen, um dich mit der Wörterbucharbeit vertraut zu machen.

Ein zweisprachiges Wörterbuch enthält folgende Informationen:
- die **Bedeutungen** eines Wortes,
- die **Aussprache** eines Wortes in **phonetischer Lautschrift**,
- die **Silbentrennung**,
- die verschiedenen **Wortklassen** (z. B. Substantiv (Nomen), Adjektiv, Verb), die meist durch Abkürzungen angezeigt werden.

homesick = *Heimweh*; salmon = *Lachs*
knee [niː], new [njuː], my [maɪ], island [ˈaɪlənd], lose [luːs]
fam-ily; home-work; bor-ing
dirty (adj. ⇨ Adjektiv), to choose (v. ⇨ Verb), book (n. ⇨ noun), trousers (pl. ⇨ Pluralwort)

Aufgepasst: Das Stichwort *(headword)* in einem Eintrag *(entry)* wird durch ein Auslassungszeichen, die **Tilde** (~), ersetzt.

hear: let me ~ from you – *lassen Sie von sich hören*
life: daily ~ – *Alltagsleben*

Zusatzinformationen im Wörterbuch

Weitere Inhalte sind:
- **grammatikalische Besonderheiten** (z. B. die unregelmäßigen Formen eines Verbs)

go, went *(past tense)*, gone *(past participle)*

- **Wendungen**

go into town – *in die Stadt gehen*, to be out of town – *nicht in der Stadt sein*

- **Beispielsätze**

place: He was placed second. – *Er wurde Zweiter.*

- **Wortzusammensetzungen**

family: family name – *Familienname*, car: car crash – *Autounfall*

- **Infokästen** zu Besonderheiten des Sprachgebrauchs oder bestimmten Themen oder hilfreiche **Bildtafeln**

useful phrases zu Themen wie "Saying thank you", "Letter-writing"

Üben

8 Englisch lernen

Übung 20

(*) Schreibe die folgenden Wörter in der richtigen alphabetischen Reihenfolge auf und schlage sie dann nach.

1. feet – fast – fashion – fan – favour – fault – fear – father

   _____

2. road – rise – ring – rink – right – ride

   _____

3. duck – dusty – dry – dummy – dying – drug

   _____

4. title – short – to – tip – near – neck – neighbour – war – underground

   _____

Übung 21

(**) Kreuze nach Kontrolle im Wörterbuch an, ob die Antwort richtig oder falsch ist. Wenn die Antwort falsch ist, verbessere sie.

	richtig	falsch
1. "advice" ist zählbar.	☐	☐
2. "to carry on" heißt „weitermachen".	☐	☐
3. "clean" ist ein Adjektiv.	☐	☐
4. "to look up" heißt „nachschlagen".	☐	☐
5. "depend" wird mit der Präposition "of" benutzt.	☐	☐
6. "platform" ist ein anderes Wort für „Bushaltestelle".	☐	☐
7. Man sagt "to make a party" und nicht "to have a party".	☐	☐

_____

_____

_____

_____

_____

Üben

8 Englisch lernen

Wissen+

Besonderheiten der englischen Aussprache	
In vielen Wörtern gibt es **stumme** Laute, die nicht gesprochen werden.	listen, often, half, walk, sandwiches, two, knuckle, answer, autumn, biscuit, hour, grandpa, climb, guest
Achte auf die richtige Aussprache von [æ] und [e].	[æ]: c**a**t, f**a**t, h**a**t, s**a**t, fl**a**t, d**a**d [e]: v**e**t, f**e**d, r**e**d, b**e**d, br**ea**d, h**ea**d
Vorsicht bei [w] und [v]: [w] wird ausgesprochen wie in *one*, [v] entspricht dem stimmhaften *w* wie in *Wasser*.	[w]: **w**eek, **w**et, **W**ednesday, **w**ith, **w**ill [v]: **v**et, e**v**ening, **v**ideo, **v**ery, se**v**en
Stimmloses oder stimmhaftes *th*? Präge dir die richtige Aussprache ein!	*stimmlos:* no**th**ing, mon**th**, **th**anks, **th**ing, mou**th**, heal**th**y; *stimmhaft:* **th**eir, **th**is, **th**ose, **th**em, toge**th**er

Übung 22

Benutze dein Wörterbuch, um die Fragen zu beantworten.

Was bedeutet "environment"? _____

Notiere die Lautschrift zu "weak", "weigh", "wilderness", "wine" und spreche sie aus. _____

_____

Welches Substantiv lässt sich von "to choose" ableiten? _____

Welche Präposition(en) benutzt man mit "to protect"? _____

Welche zusammengesetzten Substantive (Nomen) kannst du unter dem Stichwort "summer" finden? _____

Wie sagt man auf Deutsch "What's the matter?" _____

Kannst du den feststehenden Ausdruck ergänzen? "trial and _____ "

Üben

8 Englisch lernen

 Schlage die Aussprache der folgenden Wörter nach und unterstreiche den Buchstaben, der nicht ausgesprochen wird.

knife   receipt   comb   castle   climb   knee

isle   salmon   tomb   knight   nose   sword

Übung 23

 Schlage das englische Wort **bar** nach und finde jeweils die deutsche Bedeutung.

They've put bars in front of our window. ⇨ _____

We went to a bar in the centre of town. ⇨ _____

Could you get me a bar of chocolate? ⇨ _____

You have to order drinks at the bar. ⇨ _____

Übung 24

 In jedem Satz ist entweder ein falsches Wort oder eine falsche Präposition. Finde die richtige Lösung mittels eines Wörterbuches und schreibe die Sätze korrekt auf.

My mum was really worried with me.

_____

Sarah isn't at home. She is by the doctor's.

_____

This exercise is heavy.

_____

That is typical for you.

_____

We haven't been to the journey agent's yet to book our holidays.

_____

The new shop is just round the edge.

_____

This area is popular by tourists.

_____

Übung 25

Testen

8 Englisch lernen

Klassenarbeit  60 Minuten

Aufgabe 1

 Lies die folgenden drei Texte aufmerksam durch.

Yesterday Died

This is the 3rd James Colt movie and Dan Cray is starring in the role of the clever British agent. The evil guy this time is a media boss who tries to start World War III.

Colt is called in to stop him and he is helped by a highly attractive elderly lady – Miss Garble, who can still use her sword (that's why friends and foes call her "The Swordfish"). Garble is madly in love with James (also dubbed "Jamie the Heartbreaker") and although retired, she is always eager to support him.

Colt movie fans can expect all the usual action and explosions in *Yesterday Died*, but some things will be different, like Colt's car. In the other Colt movies the hero drives a British-made sports car. This time Colt will be seen cycling – it's healthier and environmentally friendly.

Mrs Pea

Mrs Pea (Sarah Soft) is normally a quiet woman. She works at the National Gallery, a famous museum in London. All she has to do is dust the expensive paintings. She has to make sure that the pictures are spotlessly clean, but most of the time she is in the broom closet, polishing her nails. She is not very good at her job and the others think that she is the laziest person who has ever worked in a museum.

Her bosses want to get rid of her. They decide to send her away on a mission to Hollywood to meet some very important people in America. And from this moment on, Mrs Pea brings chaos (and flashy colours of nail polish) to the world.

Gigantic

The true story of the ship of dreams ... the Gigantic. The unsinkable tub. The great disaster. The secret in the north Atlantic Ocean. What stories of love and tragedy wait here to be told?

A beautiful woman. A poor, good-looking man. An expensive Polex watch. A true love that nothing on earth could stop. A collision with an iceberg that no-one could imagine.

See Leo di Capulet as Matt and Sadie Leaflet as Violet in the world's biggest dramatic romance. Don't miss it – it's a real tear jerker!

Testen

8 Englisch lernen

Aufgabe 2

(*) Wortschatzarbeit – finde das Gegenteil der folgenden Wörter aus dem Text.

clever	⇔	_____
elderly	⇔	_____
quiet	⇔	_____
expensive	⇔	_____
famous	⇔	_____
important	⇔	_____
unsinkable	⇔	_____
beautiful / good-looking	⇔	_____
true	⇔	_____
poor	⇔	_____

Aufgabe 3

 Schlage folgende Wörter und Ausdrücke im Wörterbuch nach und übersetze sie ins Deutsche.

to star a second time	_____
to be called in	_____
to expect sth.	_____
to retire	_____
tear jerker	_____
to get rid of sb.	_____
to imagine sth.	_____
broom closet	_____
nail polish	_____

135

Testen

8 Englisch lernen

Aufgabe 4

★★ Schreibe alle Wörter aus den drei Texten heraus, die du verstehen kannst, weil es im Deutschen ähnliche Ausdrücke gibt.

Yesterday Died: _____

_____

Mrs Pea: _____

_____

Gigantic: _____

_____

Aufgabe 5

★★★ Mache dir Notizen zu den drei Filmen: zur Handlung, zu den Schauspielerinnen und Schauspielern, zu den Figuren. Lies dazu die Texte noch einmal und markiere die betreffenden Passagen.

○ *Yesterday Died:* _____

_____

_____

_____

○ *Mrs Pea:* _____

_____

_____

_____

○ *Gigantic:* _____

_____

_____

_____

_____

○

Testen

8 Englisch lernen

Aufgabe 6

Würdest du einen dieser Filme sehen wollen? Warum? Warum nicht? Schreibe mindestens vier Sätze auf Englisch.

_____
_____
_____
_____
_____

Aufgabe 7

Höre dir auf Track 13 das Interview an, in dem Jack von Emma interviewt wird, und beantworte anschließend die Fragen.

13

1. Why is Emma interviewing Jack?
_____
_____

2. Where has Jack just been?
_____

3. Why was he there?
_____

4. How did he contact UNEP?
_____

5. Why did he want to get involved in environmental issues?
_____
_____
_____

6. What did he do at the Youth Forum?
_____
_____

7. What did Jack decide to do after he was in Blackpool?
_____
_____

Wissen • Üben • Testen

Englisch

8. Klasse

Wissen

1 Das Passiv

1.1 Das Passiv im **present tense**

simple present

Passivformen im *present tense* werden gebildet mit einer Form von *to be* sowie dem *past participle* des Vollverbs.	I **am asked** you **are asked** he/she/it **is asked** you/we/they **are asked**
Im *simple present* lauten die Formen: *am/are/is* + *past participle*.	
Aus einem Aktivsatz wird ein Passivsatz, indem man das direkte Objekt zum Subjekt macht.	Ruby writes **a letter** („Wen oder was schreibt sie?"). ⇨ **A letter** is written („Wer oder was wird geschrieben?").
Merke: Wenn das direkte Objekt im Plural steht, muss auch das Prädikat des Passivsatzes im Plural stehen.	She feeds **her cats** twice a day. ⇨ **Her cats** are fed twice a day.
Die Person, die die Handlung verursacht, wird mit *by* angehängt **(by-agent)**.	A letter is written **by Susie**.
Der *by-agent* kann meist weggelassen werden.	The bank is robbed (by robbers).
Manche Sätze ergeben ohne *by-agent* allerdings keinen Sinn. In diesen Fällen muss der Verursacher oder die Ursache unbedingt genannt werden.	The flood is caused by heavy rain.

present progressive

Im *present progressive* lauten die Formen des Passivs *am/are/is being* + *past participle*.	I **am being asked** he/she/it **is being asked** you/we/they **are being asked**
Die *simple present*- und die *present progressive*-Formen haben im Passiv die gleiche Funktion wie im Aktiv (↗ Band 7, Kap. 4): ○ *simple present*-Formen für regelmäßige, gewohnheitsmäßige Ereignisse,	Every four years, when the summer Olympics are on, our TV is very rarely switched off.
○ *present progressive*-Formen für aktuell andauernde Ereignisse.	The Olympics are on right now. Our TV isn't being switched off easily these days.

Wissen

1 Das Passiv

Direktes und indirektes Objekt

Aufgepasst: Verben, die zwei Objekte haben, können zwei unterschiedliche Passivsätze bilden, je nachdem, ob das direkte Objekt (meist eine Sache) oder das *indirekte Objekt* (meist eine Person) in den Vordergrund der Aussage gestellt werden soll.

My daughter tells *me* a joke.
S V *indirektes Objekt* („wem?") direktes Objekt („wen oder was?")

Steht im Aktivsatz das *indirekte Objekt* im Mittelpunkt der Aussage, wird es im Passivsatz zum *Subjekt*.

I („wer oder was?") am told a joke by my daughter.

Soll das direkte Objekt hervorgehoben werden, wird dieses zum Subjekt im Passivsatz.

A joke („wer oder was?") is told to me by my daughter.

Verben mit Präpositionen

Einige englische Verben haben eine Präposition als festen Bestandteil. Werden solche Verben im Passiv gebraucht, müssen Verb und Präposition unbedingt zusammenbleiben. Zu diesen Verben gehören:

to ask for, to pay for, to complain about, to rely on, to think about, to speak about, to take care of, to talk about, to laugh at, to think of

The children **take care of** the pet. ⇨ The pet **is taken care of** (by the children).
The Millers **laugh at** the little monkey every other day. ⇨ The little monkey **is laughed at** every other day.
You can **rely on** her. ⇨ She can **be relied on**.

Aufgepasst: Wenn das Passiv einen Vorgang beschreibt, kann in der Umgangssprache auch *to get* anstelle der Form von *to be* verwendet werden.

My friend **is** always **laughed at** when she tries to say something.
Oder: My friend always **gets laughed at** when she tries to say something.

Merke: Nicht alle Verben können ein Passiv bilden! Dazu gehören:

to have, to fit, to resemble, to suit

They have a nice car. ⇨ ~~A nice car is had by them~~.
My daughter has grown. Her clothes don't fit her any longer. ⇨ ~~She is not fitted by her clothes~~.

Üben

1 Das Passiv

Übung 1

(*) Bestimme die Satzglieder.

Yulia shows her new dress to her friend.

Yulia: _____ , shows: _____ ,

her new dress: _____ , to her friend: _____

The new dress is shown to her friend.

the new dress: _____ , is shown: _____ ,

to her friend: _____

Her friend is shown the new dress.

her friend: _____ , is shown: _____ ,

the new dress: _____

Übung 2

(**) Bilde Passivsätze mit dem by-agent und schreibe sie in dein Übungsheft.

English pupils / French / often / to learn

_____
_____
_____

these stamps / to collect / my parents

_____
_____
_____

at the moment / this hit album / to make / Adele

_____
_____
_____

to present / these paintings / the Queen / every summer

_____
_____
_____

Üben

1 Das Passiv

Übung 3

Ein Buch wird veröffentlicht. Verwandle alle Sätze vom Aktiv ins Passiv.

Publishing a book
First, the author writes a story. At the publishing company the editor *(Lektor)* reads and corrects the text. At the same time the employees in book production design the book's layout. An artist illustrates the text. And finally the printers print the book and bind it. The publishing company advertises the new book in newspapers and magazines and the bookstores offer it to their customers. And last of all, somebody buys the book and reads it.

Übung 4

Smiley, Milas Hündin, ist krank. Lies dir durch, was Mila unternimmt, und setze den Text dann ins Passiv.

... takes her to the vet *(Tierarzt)* right away,
... tells the doctor about Smiley's problem,
... then takes her home again,
... watches her closely all day,
... gives her some medicine.

Üben

1 Das Passiv

Wissen⁺

Persönliches und unpersönliches Passiv

Verben des Sagens und Denkens bilden das Passiv, indem *to* + Vollverb an die Passivkonstruktion angehängt wird **(persönliches Passiv)**. Oft kann man mit „man" übersetzen.

Joe **is said to be** a liar. ⇨ **Man sagt,** Joe ist ein Lügner.
He **is said to be** ill.
She **is expected to pass** her exam brilliantly.

Wenn eine Information nicht gesichert ist, kann man das **unpersönliche Passiv** verwenden (oft in Zeitungsartikeln). Es wird gebildet mit *it,* einer Form von *to be*, dem *past participle* und *that*.

It is said that he is quite ill.
It is thought that thousands of people were killed in the floods.
It is reported that four people have been injured in the accident.

Übung 5

 Übersetze.

Man sagt, er sei sehr reich.

_____

Es wird berichtet, dass bei dem Unfall vier Menschen getötet wurden.

_____

Man behauptet von Sienna, sie sei eine gute Schülerin.

_____

Die Straßen werden jeden Tag gereinigt.

_____

Das Haus wird gerade abgerissen.

_____

Schau! Es werden gerade zwei Männer von der Polizei festgenommen.

_____

Meine Eltern werden jeden Monat von unseren Nachbarn eingeladen.

_____

Üben

1 Das Passiv

Übung 6

Übersetze die folgenden Sätze ins Englische. Achtung: Die Verben haben zwei Objekte! Vergiss den by-agent nicht, falls dieser notwendig ist.

Den Schülern werden gerade von ihrer Lehrerin viele Hausaufgaben gegeben.
___

Den Arbeitern wird gewöhnlich viel Geld bezahlt.
___

Das alte Haus wird gerade von unseren Großeltern an eine junge Familie verkauft.
___

Die Welpen (puppies) werden mir von meinem Nachbarn gezeigt.
___

Meine Freunde bekommen manchmal von mir kleine Geschenke.
___

Übung 7

Finde zu allen Sätzen aus Aufgabe 6 eine zweite Möglichkeit des Passivsatzes.

Wissen

1 Das Passiv

1.2 Das Passiv im past tense

Die Vergangenheitsformen im Passiv werden mit der entsprechenden Zeit von *to be* und dem *past participle* gebildet.	I **was told** many lies when I was a child. A movie **was being watched** at that moment.
simple past	
Im *simple past* lauten die Formen des Passivs: *was/were* + *past participle*.	I **was asked**; you **were asked**; he/she/it **was asked**; we/you/they **were asked**
Die Formen des *simple past* kennzeichnen auch im Passiv eine abgeschlossene Handlung, einen abgeschlossenen Vorgang oder einen bestimmten Zeitpunkt.	The boat was destroyed in the storm. (abgeschlossener Vorgang, denn jetzt ist das Boot zerstört)
Auch im *simple past* kann man das persönliche und das unpersönliche Passiv bilden.	He was said to be a very fast runner. It was reported that four people were injured in the accident.
past progressive	
Im *past progressive* lauten die Passivformen: *was/were being* + *past participle*.	I **was being asked**; you **were being asked**; he/she/it **was being asked**; we/you/they **were being asked**
Passivsätze im *past progressive* drücken die Gleichzeitigkeit von zwei (oder mehr) Ereignissen in der Vergangenheit aus.	I was being asked to send an application *(Bewerbung)* to a different company when the company closed.
Für Passivsätze im *simple past* und *past progressive* gelten die gleichen Regeln wie im *simple present* und *present progressive* (↗ Band 7, Kap. 4) bei	
○ zwei Objekten,	My mother told me a good joke. ⇨ I was told a good joke by my mother. / A good joke was told to me by my mother.
○ einer Präposition + Verb und	The politician gave a speech to the people. ⇨ A speech was given to the people.
○ Verben des Sagens und Denkens.	She was expected to pass her exam.
Wird eine **Frage,** die im Aktiv mit *did* gebildet wird, ins Passiv verwandelt, wird das indirekte Objekt zum neuen Subjekt des Fragesatzes, und die Form des Hilfsverbs *to be* rückt an den Satzanfang.	**Did they teach** Chinese at the international school that you attended in Shanghai? ⇨ **Was Chinese taught** at the international school that you attended in Shanghai?

Üben

1 Das Passiv

Anne ist von Kent nach London gezogen. Sie schreibt einen Brief an ihre Freundin in Kent und berichtet von den ersten Wochen. Höre dir Track 1 an und ergänze die Lücken.

1

Dear Sarah,

Hello from London! I am awfully sorry that it has taken me a while to write this letter, but I have been really busy. I had to find my way around the city, and London is really big!

However, I _____ by my new classmates.

First, I _____ our new classroom. Then, during my first week, one girl and one boy showed me around the neighbourhood.

I _____ some history of the city, too. And I _____ to join my new school's volleyball team. I _____ by the teachers, too.

I _____ a lot of questions.

My sister is quite happy here, too. On her very first day she _____ with a song. She too, _____ to join her school's sports team.

However, we also had some problems. Our newspaper _____ _____ to our house for the first three weeks and the mail _____ to our neighbours. And we _____ by our neighbours that we have to close all the windows each time my sister practises the piano! Now, after a month here in this big city, everything seems to be fine. We've done some sightseeing with our parents and _____ to a big welcoming party by my grandparents, who now live just around the block.

I'll write write another letter soon!

Take care,

Anne

Übung 8

Üben

1 Das Passiv

Übung 9

 Setze die Sätze ins Passiv des **simple past**.

Someone made this sweater in China.
_____

My husband didn't water the flowers this morning.
_____

Somebody stole my bike last summer.
_____

Did someone invite the grandparents to this concert?
_____

Fire destroyed the forests in California some years ago.
_____

We did water the grass last summer because of the drought *(Dürre)*.
_____

People spoke English all over Sweden when we travelled the country last summer.
_____

Übung 10

 Erinnerst du dich noch an die kranke Hündin Smiley in Übung 4? Berichte nun im **past tense**, was Smiley alles erlebt hat, indem du Sätze mithilfe der Stichworte aus dem Wortkasten formulierst.

~~not give her food~~ – take her to the vet **(Tierarzt)** right away – tell the doctor about Smiley's problems – take Smiley home again – watch her closely all day

Smiley *wasn't given any food. She* _____
_____
_____
_____
_____

Wissen

1 Das Passiv

1.3 Das Passiv im **present perfect** und **past perfect**

present perfect

Die Passivformen im *present perfect* werden gebildet mit *have been / has been* sowie dem *past participle* des Vollverbs.	I **have been told** a story. A story **has been written.**
Die *progressive*-Form wird nur sehr selten verwendet.	
Auch im Passiv wird das *present perfect* verwendet, wenn ein vergangenes Ereignis in die Gegenwart hinein andauert bzw. Folgen hat.	My car hasn't been cleaned yet. Our house hasn't been painted since we bought it nine years ago.
Für Passivsätze im *present perfect* gelten bei	
○ zwei Objekten,	My mother has told me a good joke. ⇨ I have been told a good joke by my mother. / A good joke has been told to me by my mother.
○ einer Präposition + Verb und	The politician has made a speech to the people. ⇨ A speech has been made to the people.
○ Verben des Sagens und Denkens die gleichen Regeln wie im *simple present* und *present progressive* (↗ Band 7, Kap. 4).	She has been expected to pass her exam brilliantly ever since she got such a good mark in the science test.
Auch im *present perfect* kann man das **persönliche** und das **unpersönliche Passiv** bilden.	She has been said to be a fine singer. It has been reported that four people were injured in the accident.

past perfect

Im *past perfect* wird das Passiv mit *had been* und dem *past participle* gebildet.	Kids **had been taught** the alphabet many years ago in first grade.
Auch im *past perfect* wird die *progressive*-Form nur äußerst selten verwendet.	
Das *past perfect* wird gewählt, um auszudrücken, dass ein Ereignis in der Vergangenheit zeitlich vor einem anderen vergangenen Ereignis liegt (↗ Band 7, Kap. 4.4).	Even though Kailey had been promised a horse she didn't get one for her birthday.

Üben

1 Das Passiv

Übung 11

Wandle die Verben ins Passiv um.

have taught ⇨ _____

has taken ⇨ _____

had sung ⇨ _____

has treated ⇨ _____

Wissen+

Verneinte Sätze im Passiv

Wird ein Satz, der mit einer Form von *do* verneint ist, ins Passiv verwandelt, so steht anstelle von *to do* eine Form des Hilfsverbs *to be*.

Tim **doesn't** feed the fish in our pond. ⇨ Our fish **aren't** fed.
Tim **didn't** feed the fish in our pond last summer. ⇨ The fish in our pond **weren't** fed last summer.

Verneinungen, die mithilfe von **to have** formuliert werden, bleiben unverändert!

He **hasn't** fed the fish yet. ⇨ The fish **haven't** been fed yet.
He **hadn't** fed the fish yet. ⇨ The fish **hadn't** been fed yet.

Übung 12

Hier geht es wieder um die Hündin Smiley aus Übung 4, diesmal aus der Perspektive von Mila. Benutze das Passiv im **present perfect,** um Fragen zu formulieren.

~~feed Smiley the right food~~ – take her out for enough walks – involve in a fight – treat her badly – not give her enough water – take her to medical check-ups often enough

Mila: "Mum, has Smiley been fed the right food?"

_____

_____

_____

_____

Üben

1 Das Passiv

Übung 13

 Verwandle die folgenden Sätze ins Passiv. Achtung: Bei zwei Sätzen gibt es zwei Möglichkeiten!

My aunt has written a poem for my birthday.
_____

Somebody had ruined the building.
_____

Lily hadn't caught the ball.
_____

Susie the cat has caught many mice over the past years.
_____

My daughter has been asking me a lot of questions the whole day.
_____
_____

He had not finished reading the newspaper article when the postman rang.
_____
_____

Amy has given us an interesting tour through San Francisco.
_____
_____

She has not broken her arm in the accident.
_____

Someone had told a boring story.
_____

Wissen

1 Das Passiv

1.4 Weitere Passivkonstruktionen

Das Passiv im *will-future*

Auch das *will-future* kann eine Passivform bilden. Sie wird gebildet mithilfe von *will be* sowie dem *past participle* des Vollverbs.

I **will be given**
he / she it **will be seen**
we / you / they **will be shown**

Das Passiv des *will-future* wird verwendet, um zukünftige, nicht beeinflussbare Ereignisse, Vermutungen und Hoffnungen sowie spontane Überlegungen auszudrücken.

Don't worry about the weather: The party will be held inside.
The film shooting *(Dreharbeiten)* is over: The movie will be released next month.

Modalverben im Passiv

Wird ein Satz, in dem ein modales Hilfsverb steht, im Passiv verwendet, so gilt:
○ Das modale Hilfsverb des Aktivsatzes (*can, must* usw.) oder die entsprechende Ersatzform (*to have to, to be able to, to be allowed to* usw.) bleibt unverändert.
○ Nur das Vollverb nimmt die Passivform an. Es steht also *to be* und das *past participle* des Vollverbs. Das modale Hilfsverb oder die entsprechende Ersatzform bleiben unverändert.

Aktiv: People must carry their suitcases to the station.
Passiv: Suitcases must be carried to the station.
Aktiv: They had to carry their suitcases upstairs.
Passiv: Their suitcases had to be carried upstairs.

Infinitivkonstruktionen im Passiv

Auch Infinitivkonstruktionen können im Passiv verwendet werden.

Our baby loves to be talked to (*Präsens*).
The parents ought to have been informed (*Perfekt*) about their son's bad school report.

Steht *to be* + Passiv, wird damit eine Anweisung ausgedrückt.

The grass isn't to be walked on.

Sätze, in denen eine *-ing*-Form des Vollverbs z. B. in Funktion eines Objekts verwendet wird, können ebenfalls im Passiv stehen.

She likes being invited (*Präsens*) to a restaurant.
I remember having been invited (*Perfekt*) to dinner before.

Üben

1 Das Passiv

Übung 14

Bilde von den angegebenen Verben die Passivformen im **will-future**.

to keep ⇨ _____

to sell ⇨ _____

to speak ⇨ _____

not to hurt ⇨ _____

Übung 15

Smiley hat Nachwuchs bekommen. Mila schenkt ihrer Freundin Sadie ein Hundebaby. Sadie sagt ihrem neuen Hund, was geschehen wird.

> ~~regular walks / take out~~ – plenty of water and food / to give – I treat you well – regular check-ups at the vet's / to take – all members of the family love you

Sadie: "You will be taken out for regular walks."

_____

_____

_____

_____

Übung 16

Wandle die Sätze vom Aktiv ins Passiv.

A football game

The team must follow the rules.

_____

All members of the team have to wear their team shirt.

_____

The goalkeeper ought to keep the goal clear.

_____

Üben

1 Das Passiv

Wissen+

Verwendung des Passivs

Für alle Passivkonstruktionen, egal in welcher Zeitform sie stehen, gilt: Sie werden besonders häufig angewendet, wenn es sich um wissenschaftliche Feststellungen oder Aussagen handelt.

The Aztec temples in Mexico **were built** hundreds of years ago.
A lot of books **have been written** about food.

Übung 17 Robert hat ein Poster mit Regeln fürs Klassenzimmer gestaltet. Setze die angegebenen Verben ins Passiv und ergänze das passende modale Hilfsverb wie z. B. **can, must, ought to, shall, should**.

All teachers and pupils _____ (to treat) with respect by all pupils.

All living creatures in this room, including spiders and all kinds of bugs *(Käfer)*, _____ (to take out) of the room alive!

Forgotten items _____ (not/to rearrange) by anybody.

All kinds of constructions _____ (to regard) as a piece of art.

Homework _____ (to avoid) as often as possible! – If homework _____ (not/to avoid), team work _____ (to accept).

Please remember: All pupils don't like to be tested! And all marks _____ (to give) fairly and generously!

Wissen

1.5 Die Zeitformen des Verbs im Aktiv und im Passiv

Verwendung / Bildung

In einem Aktivsatz führt das Subjekt eine Handlung aus. Passivsätze werden verwendet, wenn mit dem Subjekt etwas geschieht. Im Passivsatz wird oftmals nicht erwähnt, wer etwas tut. Vielmehr steht die Person oder die Sache, mit der etwas geschieht, im Vordergrund. Das Passiv wird mit einer Form des Hilfsverbs *to be* und dem Partizip Perfekt gebildet.

Gegenwart

- **simple present**
  - Aktiv: *I sing a song.*
  - Passiv: *am / is / are* + past participle
    A song is sung.
- **present progressive**
  - Aktiv: *I'm singing a song.*
  - Passiv: *am / is / are being* + past participle
    A song is being sung.

Allgemeine Aussagen, Gewohnheiten, Dauer- und Normalzustände, aufeinanderfolgende, abgeschlossene Handlungen

gerade stattfindende Handlungen

Vollendete Gegenwart

- **present perfect simple**
  - Aktiv: *I have sung a song.*
  - Passiv: *has / have been* + past participle
    A song has been sung.
- **present perfect progressive**
  - Aktiv: *I have been singing a song.*
  - Passiv: *has / have been beeing* + past participle
    A song has been being sung.

Vergangenheitshandlungen zu einer unbekannten Zeit oder mit Gegenwarts- oder Zukunftsbedeutung

in der Gegenwart noch andauernde Handlungen
wird nur selten verwendet

Zukunft

- **going to-future**
  - Aktiv: *I'm going to sing a song.*
  - Passiv: *is / are going to be* + past participle
    A song is going to be sung.
- **will-future**
  - Aktiv: *I will sing a song.*
  - Passiv: *will be* + past participle
    A song will be sung.
- **will-future progressive**
  - Aktiv: *I will be singing a song.*
  - Passiv: *will be being* + past participle
    A song will be being sung.

zukünftige Absichten, sehr wahrscheinliches Zukunftsgeschehen

allgemeine Aussagen, Vorhersagen, Vermutungen, spontane Äußerungen, Bitten, Fragen

routinemäßiges Geschehen

Wissen

Die Zeitformen des Verbs im Aktiv und im Passiv

Vergangenheit
- **simple past**
  - Aktiv: *I sang a song.*
  - Passiv: *was / were* + past participle
    A song was sung.
- **past progressive**
  - Aktiv: *I was singing a song.*
  - Passiv: *was / were being* + past participle
    A song was being sung.

Vergangenheitshandlungen zu einer bestimmten Zeit

länger andauernde Handlungen der Vergangenheit, Hintergrundhandlung oder -geschehen

Vollendete Vergangenheit
- **past perfect simple**
  - Aktiv: *I had sung a song.*
  - Passiv: *had been* + past participle
    A song had been sung.
- **past perfect progressive**
  - Aktiv: *I had been singing a song.*
  - Passiv: *had been beeing* + past participle
    A song had been being sung.

vor einem Zeitpunkt in der Vergangenheit geschehene Handlungen

bis zu einem Zeitpunkt in der Vergangenheit andauernde Handlungen
wird nur selten verwendet

Vollendete Zukunft
- **future perfect**
  - Aktiv: *I will have sung a song.*
  - Passiv: *will have been* + past participle
    A song will have been sung.

in der Zukunft vollendetes Handeln

Möglichkeitsform
- **conditional I**
  - Aktiv: *I would sing a song.*
  - Passiv: *would be* + past participle
    A song would be sung.
- **conditional II**
  - Aktiv: *I would have sung a song.*
  - Passiv: *would have been* + past participle
    A song would have been sung.

mögliches Handeln

früher, aber jetzt nicht mehr mögliches Handeln

Testen

1 Das Passiv

Klassenarbeit 1 — 60 Minuten

Aufgabe 1

Bestimme Person, Numerus (Zahl), Tempus (Zeit) und Modus (Aktiv oder Passiv).

he is asked	_____
they are being asked	_____
we have asked	_____
it will be watched	_____
they were not watered	_____
we have been watched	_____
it had been promised	_____

Aufgabe 2

Unterstreiche die verschiedenen Passivformen.

Our school magazine is not published twice a year but every three months. Look! Our latest edition is just being sold. However, it takes a lot of work to finish each edition. A lot of things have to be checked: What's going on at school that's important? Is there anything special that needs to be covered? Who is to write an article on which topic? How do we finance our magazine? Are there some companies in our city that can be asked to sponsor us? But the most important question of all is: What can we do so that as many pupils as possible are attracted?

Aufgabe 3

Wenn Jay und seine Familie in Urlaub fahren, verpflichten sie sich, die folgenden Regeln einzuhalten. Verwende **to be** + Passiv.

Big cities _____ (to avoid).

Every second ice cream parlour _____ (to visit).

Game consoles _____ (not/to take) out of the car.

Testen

1 Das Passiv

Aufgabe 4

Im vergangenen Jahr gab es ebenfalls Regeln. Setze das **simple past** von „müssen" ein.

All playgrounds _____ (to visit) for 30 minutes at least.

Stuffed animals _____ (to take) to all places of interest, too.

Of course, traffic jams _____ (to bypass) then, too.

Camping sites _____ (to prefer) to expensive, fancy hotels because of the children.

Aufgabe 5

Wandle die Sätze vom Aktiv ins Passiv um. Achtung: Manchmal gibt es zwei Möglichkeiten!

A thief stole my camera.
_____
_____

The children are eating some ice cream.
_____
_____

Phil gave me a book for my birthday.
_____
_____

The teacher didn't ask me a lot of questions.
_____
_____

Grandfather gave me some extra pocket money.
_____
_____

Testen

1 Das Passiv

Aufgabe 6

Setze die richtige Zeit in die Lücken: **simple present, present progressive** oder **simple past**?

Many toys _____ (to make) of plastic.

The apples are ripe. They _____ (have/to pick) by somebody.

A century ago, most wedding announcements _____ (to write) by hand. Today, very few wedding announcements _____ _____ (to write) by hand.

I have got to walk to work today. My car _____ (to steal) last week.

Look! The famous actress _____ (to introduce) to the Mayor of the city at the moment.

The first usable electrical light bulb _____ (to invent) by Thomas Alva Edison.

Aufgabe 7

Übersetze.

Soeben wird die Bank überfallen.

_____

Der kleine Junge wird von seinen Freunden ausgelacht.

_____

Welche Fotos können in unserer Schülerzeitung veröffentlicht werden?

_____

Letztes Jahr wurde mir kein sehr guter Job angeboten.

_____

Vor langer Zeit wurde Poppy ein Pferd versprochen. Das Pferd wurde heute auf ihre Farm gebracht.

_____

Testen

1 Das Passiv

Aufgabe 8

 Erzähle zu einem der drei Bilder eine kurze Geschichte: Bilde mindestens fünf Sätze im Passiv.

I am a poor flower.
I was picked by an ugly man.
Then I was taken into a hot car.
I wasn't given any water …

_____
_____
_____
_____
_____

I am a happy pony.
I am treated well by my owner, a girl named Lea …

_____
_____
_____
_____
_____

I am a fast red car.
I get washed every Saturday.
My engine is checked regularly …

_____
_____
_____
_____
_____

Testen

1 Das Passiv

Klassenarbeit 2 — 60 Minuten

Aufgabe 9

Ergänze die Tabelle. Schreibe vollständige Sätze. Achte darauf, jeweils passende Signalwörter zu verwenden, wenn nötig.

simple present	present perfect simple	will-future
A movie is watched every Saturday.		
	The door has been shut.	
		The book will be sold out quickly.
Football is played all over the world.		

Aufgabe 10

Wähle das richtige Verb aus dem Wortkasten und setze es im Passiv in die Sätze ein. Wähle das **simple present**.

> to cut down – to encourage – to take – to speak – to pollute – to visit

Injured people _____ to hospitals by ambulances.

Sometimes trees _____ in forests.

English _____ in Ireland.

London _____ by many tourists every year.

Pupils all over the world _____ to learn foreign languages.

Testen

1 Das Passiv

Aufgabe 11

 Vervollständige die Sätze. Achte auf den richtigen Gebrauch der Zeiten.

These shoes _____ (to make) in China.

Too much nonsense _____ (to show) on TV.

Dairy products *(Milchprodukte)* _____ (should/to keep) in a fridge.

More than 5,000 tickets _____ (to sell) for the pop concert in London.

The book *Charlie and the Chocolate Factory* _____ (to write) by Roald Dahl in 1964.

Aufgabe 12

 Setze die angegebenen Sätze ins Passiv; den **by-agent** musst du nicht angeben.

They never offer free books to students.

_____

So far, nobody has taught the five-year-old twins swimming.

_____

Pupils must solve a lot of maths exercises at school.

_____

The Normans invaded Britain in 1066.

_____

Aufgabe 13

Aktiv oder Passiv? Setze die angegebenen Verben in die richtige Form und achte auf den richtigen Gebrauch der Zeiten.

Times are a-changing

At the beginning of the 20th century, many things _____ (to change). Farmers started to use machines, and between 1901 and 1905, US wheat fields _____ (to cut) with machines for the first time. Instant coffee _____ (to invent). Women _____ (to start) to change the way they dressed and skirts _____ (to become) shorter. In the late 1920's, the first sound films _____ (to show) in American cinemas. In

Testen

1 Das Passiv

1929, the first Coca-Cola bottle _____ (to sell) in Germany and millions of bottles _____ (to drink) ever since. In 1945, the microwave oven _____ (to invent) and since then people _____ (to spend) less time in the kitchen. Nowadays, it _____ (to say) that in some big cities, apartments _____ (to build) without kitchens. Fast food, however, has a lot of calories and some doctors say that fast food _____ (not/to eat).

More technical innovations _____ (to influence) our daily routine after World War II: The colour TV _____ (to become) popular and the internet as well as mobile phones _____ (to revolutionize) human communication. Today's youngsters will sure live on to experience that even more inventions _____ (to make) in the forthcoming years.

So what about you? Can you _____ (to imagine) the future?

Aufgabe 14

*** Übersetze.

Man kann sich auf ihn leider gar nicht verlassen.
_____

Zum Glück wurde bei dem Unfall niemand verletzt.
_____

Die Zeitungen berichten, dass Hunderte von Menschen in den Fluten zu Tode kamen.
_____
_____

Man hat dem Kind ein Pferd versprochen.
_____

Das Buch wurde von der Klasse mit Begeisterung gelesen.
_____

Der Job wurde Kailey angeboten, nicht Mila.
_____

Wissen

2 Die indirekte Rede

2.1 Die Veränderung der Personal- und Possessivpronomen

Direkte und indirekte Rede

Die **direkte** oder **wörtliche Rede** gibt die Aussagen, Ansichten oder Meinungen einer Person wörtlich wieder.	The teacher says: "Hurry up. The bell is ringing in two minutes."
Merke: In der direkten Rede kennzeichnen **Anführungszeichen** die Aussage.	Sarah asks her friend: "Did you notice Mrs Pinnock's new haircut?" Dad agrees: "I'll pay for your new bike."
Durch die **indirekte Rede** *(reported speech)* wird eine Aussage, Ansicht oder Meinung einem Dritten mitgeteilt. Am Anfang steht ein **einleitendes Verb**, auf das oft eine Konjunktion (etwa *that – dass, if / whether – ob*) folgt.	Phil **says that** he doesn't like Mondays. Sarah **tells her** mum **that** she has finished her homework. Murat **wonders whether** his girlfriend likes strawberry ice cream.
Vor dem *that*-Satz steht kein Komma. *That* kann auch weggelassen werden.	He says the sea is too cold to go for a swim.
Verben, die die indirekte Rede einleiten, nennt man *reporting verbs*. Dazu zählen: *to say, to tell, to ask, to wonder, to answer, to think, to report, to mention*	He answers that he likes chocolate. Nick mentions that he prefers coke to milk.

Veränderung der Pronomen

Bei der Wiedergabe der direkten in der indirekten Rede werden u. a. die Pronomen verändert.

Mila: "**I** walk **my** dog every day." ⇨ Mila says that **she** walks **her** dog every day.

Für die **Personalpronomen** gilt:
I, you ⇨ he, she
we, you ⇨ they
me, you ⇨ him, her
us, you ⇨ them

Liam: "**We** live on Main Street." ⇨ Liam says that **they** live on Main Street.

Für die **Possessivpronomen** gilt:
my, your ⇨ his, her
our, your ⇨ their

Chan and Lea: "Tim and Matteo are **our** friends." ⇨ Chan and Lea say that Tim and Matteo are **their** friends.

Üben

2 Die indirekte Rede

Übung 1

 Trage die fehlenden Pronomen in die Sätze in der indirekten Rede ein.

Ava complains: "I don't like homework."

Ava complains that __she__ doesn't like homework.

The mother to her children: "I won't give you any more chocolate."

The mother tells her children that _____ won't give _____ any more chocolate.

Tom to Paula: "I saw you in town yesterday but I think you didn't see me."

Tom tells Paula that _____ saw _____ in town the day before but _____ thinks that _____ didn't see _____.

Helen asks Mei: "Are you good at swimming?"

Helen asks Mei if _____ is good at swimming.

Laura to her mum: "Do you know where my mobile phone is?"

Laura asks her mum if _____ knows where _____ mobile phone is.

Matt and Mei to Noah: "We won't come to your party on Friday."

Matt and Mei inform Noah that _____ won't come to _____ party on Friday.

Wissen⁺

Keine Veränderung der Pronomen

Wenn ein Sprecher seine eigene Aussage wiedergibt, dann bleibt das Personalpronomen unverändert.	Father to Tim: "I will wash the car now." Father to Tim: "Go inside and tell your mother that **I** will wash the car."
Achtung: Wenn ein Sprecher etwas berichtet, das er selbst erlebt hat, dann ändern sich die Pronomen wie folgt: *you* ⇨ *I* (Personalpronomen) *your* ⇨ *my* (Possessivpronomen)	The policeman asks me: "Where do **you** live?" ⇨ The policeman asks me where **I** live. The teacher asks me: "Where's **your** homework?" ⇨ The teacher asks me where **my** homework is.

Wissen

2 Die indirekte Rede

2.2 Der Gebrauch der Zeiten

Für die korrekte Wiedergabe eines englischen Satzes in der indirekten Rede ist das **einleitende Verb** *(reporting verb)* wichtig: Steht es in der **Gegenwart** *(present tense)*, bleibt die Zeitform des wiederzugebenden Verbs unverändert; nur die Pronomen erfahren eine Verschiebung.

Paul: "I **love** chocolate." ⇨ Paul says that he **loves** chocolate.
Chan: "I **haven't seen** my sister for ages." ⇨ Chan says that she **hasn't seen** her sister for ages.

Steht allerdings das **einleitende Verb** in der **Vergangenheit** *(past tense)*, dann erfährt das Verb in der indirekten Rede eine zeitliche Verschiebung. Dabei gilt:

direkte Rede	⇨	indirekte Rede
present tense	⇨	past tense (1)
present perfect	⇨	past perfect (2)
past tense	⇨	past perfect (3)
going to-future	⇨	was / were going to + infinitive (4)
will-future	⇨	would + infinitive (5)

Maurice: "I **like** cycling." ⇨ Maurice said that he **liked** cycling. (1)
Lea: "I **haven't been** to the supermarket." ⇨ Lea said that she **hadn't been** to the supermarket. (2)
Charles: "I **didn't go** to the party last Friday." ⇨ Charles said that he **hadn't gone** to the party the previous Friday. (3)
Ivy: "I'm **going to buy** a book tomorrow." ⇨ Ivy said that she **was going to buy** a book the next day. (4)
Kieran: "I **will do** it straight away." ⇨ Kieran said that he **would do** it straight away. (5)

Merke: Bei der Verwendung von *progressive*-Formen gelten dieselben Regeln!

is watching ⇨ was watching
have been watching ⇨ had been watching

Steht das *reporting verb* im *past tense*, findet auch bei **Orts- und Zeitangaben** eine Verschiebung statt:

direkte Rede	⇨	indirekte Rede
now	⇨	then / at the moment
today	⇨	on that day
tonight	⇨	that night
tomorrow	⇨	the next / the following day
yesterday	⇨	the day before / the previous day
last month	⇨	the month before / the previous month
next year	⇨	the following year
this	⇨	that
here	⇨	there

Ethan: "It's my mum's birthday **today**." ⇨ Ethan said that it was his mum's birthday **on that day**.
She said: "I'm going to have my birthday party **here**." ⇨ She said that she was going to have her birthday party **there**.

Üben

2 Die indirekte Rede

 Unterstreiche die richtige Verbform.

Mia: "I went to the cinema yesterday."
Mia says that she goes / went / had gone to the cinema the day before.

Laura: "I hate school."
Laura said that she hates / hated / will hate school.

Henry: "I won't go to school tomorrow."
Henry said that he won't go / would have gone / would not go to school the following day.

Yosef: "I'm going to listen to my favourite music all day."
Yosef said that he was going to listen / is going to listen / had listened to his favourite music all day.

Zoe: "I haven't visited grandma for ages."
Zoe said that she hasn't visited / won't visit / hadn't visited grandma for ages.

Übung 2

 Schreibe die Sätze in der indirekten Rede in dein Heft.

Tom said: "I will do my homework tomorrow."
Lily told her mother: "I saw a wonderful dress at my favourite shop today."
Paul tells his friend: "I'm going to go to England on holiday this year."
Liam asked: "Have you ever been to the United States?"
Deniz told her friend: "Yesterday the rain stopped in the afternoon."

Übung 3

Wissen+

Keine Zeitverschiebung Steht die direkte Rede bereits im *past perfect*, erfolgt keine zeitliche Verschiebung.	The children: "We **hadn't finished** our maths test when the bell rang." ⇨ The children said that they **hadn't finished** their maths test when the bell rang.
Ist eine Aussage allgemein gültig, bleibt das Verb in der indirekten Rede auch dann unverändert, wenn das einleitende Verb in der Vergangenheit steht.	The teacher: "Berlin **is** the capital of Germany." ⇨ The teacher **said** that Berlin **is** the capital of Germany.
Bei einem längeren Bericht (z. B. im Fernsehen oder einem Artikel) wird häufig nur das erste Verb aus der direkten Rede *(past form)* in der indirekten Rede ins *past perfect* gesetzt. Auch das *reporting verb* steht in dem Fall nur im ersten Satz.	A policeman said that there **had been** a terrible accident yesterday. Two people were injured. The ambulance only arrived half an hour later when one of the men was already dead.

Üben

2 Die indirekte Rede

Übung 4

Lily und Camille telefonieren. Später erzählt Camille ihrer Mutter, was Lily gesagt hat. Setze Lilys Worte in die indirekte Rede. Kontrolliere deine Lösung mithilfe von Track 2.

2

> "Camille, I'm very sorry that I didn't call earlier. The reason is that there was a theatre performance at school this morning. The performance was very nice. Everybody was watching the stage when the fire-alarm set off and suddenly, all the people were running towards the exit. I slipped, fell down and broke my leg. So I'm in hospital now and won't go to school tomorrow, either."

Camille tells her mother: "Lily called. She told me

Üben

2 Die indirekte Rede

Übung 5

 Sage auf die folgenden Aussagen immer das Gegenteil, indem du die Sätze jeweils mit **I thought you said** einleitest.

This snack bar is expensive. ⇨ <u>Is it? I thought you said it was cheap.</u>

Ann isn't coming to the party on Saturday. ⇨ Really? _____

_____.

Helen likes Paul. ⇨ Does she? _____

_____.

I'll be in London on Monday. ⇨ Will you? _____

_____ in Manchester.

I can speak a little French. ⇨ Can you? _____

_____.

I haven't been to the cinema for ages. ⇨ Haven't you? _____

_____ last Sunday.

Übung 6

Setze die Verben in den Klammern in die richtige Zeit. Achte darauf, dass es sich bei den Sätzen um die indirekte Rede handelt!

Some pupils were talking about homework. One boy said he _____

_____ (to do) homework for three hours every evening. Some pupils

also said that they _____ (not – to do) their homework yet.

Vicky told her teacher that she _____ (to feel) ill.

Leo said that he _____ (to phone) his mother from York.

Mrs Hall told me that Ted and Mia _____ (to be) at their aunt's.

Leila told Jim that he _____ (may see) her at Becky's party.

Üben

2 Die indirekte Rede

Übung 7

*** Übersetze.

Lily sagte, dass die Theatervorstellung sehr gut gewesen sei.

_____

Camille erzählte uns, dass Lily nun einen Gipsverband *(cast)* am Bein habe.

_____

Mrs Miller sagte, dass Lily noch immer zu krank sei, um in die Schule zu gehen.

_____

Der Arzt sagte, er werde alles tun, um Lily zu helfen.

_____

Lilys Mutter erzählte, dass sie in den Ferien nun nicht zum Skilaufen fahren würden.

_____

Übung 8

*** Streiche die Fehler in den folgenden Sätzen an. Schreibe dann jeweils den ganzen verbesserten Satz auf.

My cousin said he will meet me in front of the restaurant.

_____

Rico told James that he is going to buy a new computer.

_____

Mr Dixon said he hasn't been to the cinema since 2009.

_____

George told me that he can help with my English homework.

_____

Wissen

2 Die indirekte Rede

2.3 Die Wiedergabe von Fragen und Befehlen

Fragesätze

Auch indirekte **Fragesätze** werden durch ein *reporting verb (to ask, to want to know)* eingeleitet. Dabei gilt:
- Die Veränderungen der Pronomen und die Zeitverschiebung folgt den entsprechenden Regeln der indirekten Rede für den Aussagesatz (↗ Kap. 2.1 und 2.2).

Amy: "When **did** Luca **leave** the party?" ⇨ Amy wanted to know when Luca **had left** the party.

- Am Ende einer indirekten Frage steht **kein** Fragezeichen.
- Die Satzstellung in der indirekten Frage ist wie im Aussagesatz: S(ubjekt) – V(erb) – O(bjekt).

Mum: "Alma, **have** you **finished** your homework?" ⇨ Mum asked **whether** Alma (S) **had finished** (V) her homework (O).

Bei Fragesätzen, die mit einem **Fragewort** (z.B. *who, when, where*) eingeleitet werden, steht dasselbe Fragewort auch im indirekten Fragesatz.

Livia: "**Where** are my new trousers?" ⇨ Livia asked **where** her new trousers were.

Aufgepasst: Fragesätze, in denen die Fragewörter *what, who, where* oder *which* mit dem Hilfsverb *to be* kombiniert sind, können eine vom Schema S – V – O abweichende Wortstellung haben.

Annie: "What's the matter?" ⇨ Annie asked what was the matter.
Oder: Annie asked what the matter was.

Fragesätze, die ohne ein Fragewort auskommen, werden in der indirekten Frage mit *if* oder *whether* formuliert.

Livia: "Mum, did you see my new trousers?" ⇨ Livia wanted to know **if / whether** her mum had seen her new trousers.

Befehle und Aufforderungen

Befehle oder Aufforderungen in der indirekten Rede werden im Englischen mit einem **Infinitiv mit *to*** wiedergegeben. Als einleitendes Verb stehen meist *to order* oder *to tell*.

The teacher to his pupils: "Copy the text." ⇨ The teacher **told** his pupils **to copy** the text.

Auch für die indirekte Wiedergabe eines Angebots, einer Einladung oder einer Bitte wird ein Infinitiv mit *to* verwendet.

James: "I'll babysit Maya and Milo tonight." ⇨ **James promised to babysit** Maya and Milo that night.

Üben

2 Die indirekte Rede

Übung 9

Livia und ihre Freundinnen sind Mitglieder der Schulmannschaft im Rudern. Zurück von einem Wettkampf am Wochenende stellt ihnen die Klasse viele Fragen. Formuliere diese Fragen in indirekte Rede um.

What kind of sports competition was it?
_____

Where did the competition take place?
_____

Why are five people in a team?
_____

Which distance did your race cover?
_____

Who won the race?
_____

Übung 10

Setze die folgenden Sätze in die indirekte Rede.

Cillian asks you: "Are you good at football?"
Cillian asked if/whether I _____.

Ben: "Kieran, do your parents like movies?"
Ben asked _____.

Evan: "Dylan, have you ever tried to write a weblog?"
Evan wanted to know _____.

Dylan: "Will you travel to Germany next summer, Sean?"
Dylan asked _____.

Sara asks you: "Do you like Mexican food?"
Sara asks _____.

Mum: "Have you practised enough for your concert, Laura?"
Mum wanted to know _____.

Mother to her daughter: "Lay the table, Lily!"
_____.

Üben

2 Die indirekte Rede

Übung 11

 Ihr habt einen neuen Englischlehrer. Schreib deiner amerikanischen Freundin eine Mail, in der du ihr mitteilst, auf welche Regeln ihr euch geeinigt habt. Verwende als einleitendes Verb **to promise / to agree** oder **to be obliged** (verpflichtet sein).

Beispiel: Don't be late for lessons! ⇨ We agreed not to be late for lessons.

Classroom rules

Take out your books for each subject right at the beginning of every lesson!

Don't talk to your neighbour!

Ask correct and complete questions!

Don't fight with your classmates!

Be quiet when somebody else is speaking!

Be polite to each other!

Help your classmates when necessary!

Üben

2 Die indirekte Rede

Übung 12

 Mr Stevenson stellt Fragen und macht Aussagen. Verwandle sie in indirekte Rede mit den einleitenden Verben im **simple past**.

1. Someone left the windows open last Monday.

2. Who can get the register tomorrow?

3. Where did Phil put the sponge yesterday?

4. Why wasn't there any chalk two days ago?

5. Yulia, present your project next week!

6. How was your geography excursion last week?

Mr Stevenson asked / said / told …

_____
_____
_____
_____
_____
_____
_____
_____
_____
_____
_____

Wissen

2 Die indirekte Rede

2.4 Modale Hilfsverben in der indirekten Rede

Das modale Hilfsverb **can** wird in der indirekten Rede zu *could*.	Tom: "I **can** earn some extra cash by helping my father." ⇨ Tom explained that he **could** earn some extra cash by helping his father.
May wird bei der Wiedergabe zu *might*.	Mother: "I may need some help." ⇨ Mother said she might need some help.
Das modale Hilfsverb **must** ○ kann unverändert bleiben, wenn ein Vorschlag, eine Annahme oder eine Schlussfolgerung ausgedrückt werden, ○ wird durch *had to* ersetzt, wenn es eine Verpflichtung ausdrückt.	Marc: "You must be Lisa's mother." ⇨ Marc said that she must be Lisa's mother. *(Schlussfolgerung)* Teacher: "You must bring your parent's signature." ⇨ The teacher said that we had to bring our parent's signature. *(Verpflichtung)*
Für das modale Hilfsverb **mustn't** gilt in der indirekten Rede: ○ Es bleibt entweder unverändert oder ○ es wird durch *shouldn't / wasn't to / weren't to* ersetzt.	Mum: "You mustn't eat so much chocolate." ⇨ Mum said that I mustn't / shouldn't / wasn't to / weren't to eat so much chocolate.
Das modale Hilfsverb **needn't** bleibt ○ entweder unverändert oder ○ wird durch *didn't have to* ersetzt.	Teacher: "You needn't copy the text because of your broken arm." ⇨ The teacher told me that I needn't / didn't have to copy the text because of my broken arm.
Das modale Hilfsverb **shall** (in der 1. Person) bleibt in der indirekten Rede ○ unverändert oder ○ wird mit *would* wiedergegeben.	The Millers: "We shall be delighted to meet your daughter." ⇨ The Millers said that they shall be / would be delighted to meet our daughter.
Merke: Die modalen Hilfsverben *would, could, might, should* und *ought to* bleiben unverändert.	Jamie: "I would buy the ring if I could." ⇨ Jamie said he would buy the ring if he could.

Üben

2 Die indirekte Rede

Übung 13

Jeweils eines der drei Modalverben muss seine Form ändern, wenn das **reporting verb** im **past tense** steht. Unterstreiche es jeweils.

might / would / can   must / may / should

could / might / will   shall / would / must

Übung 14

Tim und Annie haben letzte Woche besprochen, was sie an ihrem 15. Hochzeitstag unternehmen wollen. Ihre Tochter Sarah hat das Gespräch belauscht und schreibt nun ihrem Bruder davon. Achte besonders auf die Modalverben in der indirekten Rede.

Tim: "It's our fifteenth wedding anniversary next Saturday. Shall we go out for dinner together?"

Dad asked mum whether / if _____

_____ .

Annie: "Well, yes. But what shall we do with the baby?"

But mum wanted to know what _____

_____ .

Tim: "Maybe Sarah or her brother can babysit?"

Dad suggested that _____

_____ .

Annie: "That's a good idea. But where shall we go to?"

Mum agreed and asked _____ .

Tim: "We might go to the Mexican restaurant near City Hall *(Rathaus)*?

Dad said that _____

_____ .

Annie: "I'm looking forward to Saturday evening!"

Mum said that _____ .

Üben

2 Die indirekte Rede

Übung 15

 Setze die Aussagen in die indirekte Rede. Verwende **reporting verbs** aus dem Wortkasten. Achte darauf, bei Bitten und Aufforderungen den Infinitiv mit **to** zu verwenden.

> to reply – to ask – to say – to tell – to explain – to agree

It is Saturday afternoon. The Ackers are *(present tense)* in their kitchen.

Mrs Acker: "Tom, have you done the weekend shopping yet?"

_____

Mr Acker: "No, I haven't."

_____

Mrs Acker: "Well, you must hurry up, the supermarket closes in half an hour."

_____

Mr Acker: "Okay, I'll go now. What do we need?"

_____

Mrs Acker: "Would you please bring potatoes, sausages, beans and some milk?"

_____

Mr Acker, sighing: "I hope I won't forget anything."

_____

Übung 16

Nun ist es Sonntag. Mrs Acker berichtet ihrer Freundin am Telefon von der gestrigen Unterhaltung mit ihrem Mann. Verwende dieses Mal durchgehend **reporting verbs** im **past tense**.

> "Yesterday, we were in our kitchen. I asked Tom whether _____
> _____
> _____
> _____
> _____
> _____."

Testen

2 Die indirekte Rede

Klassenarbeit 1 — 45 Minuten

Aufgabe 1

Trage die entsprechenden Zeit- und Ortsadverbien ein.

direkte Rede	indirekte Rede
	then
today	
last month	
	that
next year	
	there
tomorrow	

Aufgabe 2

Wähle die richtige Verbform.

"Last night I had a wonderful dream of a beautiful woman."

He told his friend that he _____ a wonderful dream.

☐ had gotten   ☐ has had   ☐ had had

"I will do everything to help you."

He said that he _____ do everything to help his friend.

☐ might   ☐ would   ☐ could

"Our teacher gave us a test yesterday."

She told me that their teacher _____ a test the other day.

☐ had given them   ☐ had them given   ☐ had given us

Testen

2 Die indirekte Rede

Aufgabe 3 (*)

Ergänze jeweils das richtige Pronomen.

Cara asks Jack: "Are you good at dancing?"

Cara asks Jack if _____ is good at dancing.

A woman asked Grace: "Have you seen our dog lately?"

A woman asked Grace if _____ had seen _____ dog lately.

"I had a terrible accident last week and my arm is broken."

He said that _____ had had a terrible accident the week before and _____ arm was broken.

Joe asked his friend Hanif: "Can you give me your homework on Monday?"

Joe wanted to know from me if _____ could give _____ homework on Monday.

Caleb told his father: "I saw you kissing your secretary yesterday but I think you didn't notice me."

Caleb told his father that _____ had seen _____ kissing _____ secretary the day before but _____ thought _____ had not noticed _____ .

Aufgabe 4 (**)

Wandle die Sätze in die indirekte Rede um.

Mum: "Get up! You mustn't sleep in."

Mum told me _____

Paul: "It would be nice if I could take you out for dinner, Maya."

_____

Father: "You needn't pretend *(so tun als ob)* to be rich."

_____

Mum: "You need to take care of your sister while I am be at the dentist's."

_____

179

Testen

2 Die indirekte Rede

Aufgabe 5

 Übersetze.

Mutter sagte, dass sie morgen nach San Francisco fliegen würde.
_____

Der Lehrer fragte, wer uns diese Geschichte erzählt hätte.
_____

Sie sagten, sie hätten zwei Wochen auf Mallorca verbracht.
_____

Vater schlug vor, das Fußballspiel im Fernsehen anzusehen.
_____

Er fragte mich, ob ich wüsste, wie viel Uhr es ist.
_____

Die Kinder sagten, sie leben schon seit vier Jahren in diesem Haus.
_____

Meine Tochter wollte wissen, wer mir von ihrer schlechten Note erzählt hatte.
_____

Das Mädchen sagte, sie esse gerade Schokolade.
_____

Aufgabe 6

 Setze die folgenden Sätze in die indirekte Rede. Achte auf das einleitende Verb!

George: "My sister has had a new car for two weeks."
George said _____.

Sarah: "I don't like fish."
Sarah has just told me _____.

Mr Dexter: "I have never spoken to Jane's teacher."
Mr Dexter explained to his wife that _____.

The policeman: "Some drivers can be really careless."
The policeman explains to us that _____.

Ivy: "After I had come home from school, I had something to eat."
Ivy said that _____.

Testen

2 Die indirekte Rede

Klassenarbeit 2  45 Minuten

Aufgabe 7

Von der direkten zur indirekten Rede ändern sich die Pronomen. Ergänze die Tabelle.

direct speech	indirect speech	Art des Pronomens
I	she/he	Personalpronomen
my		
	them	
	him/her	
you		Personalpronomen
our		Possessivpronomen

Aufgabe 8

Trage die fehlenden Pronomen in der indirekten Rede ein.

Jasper: "I have met a wonderful girl. I feel very happy at the moment."

Jasper says that __he__ has met a wonderful girl and that __he__ feels very happy at the moment.

Grandmother: "I won't go to church today because I feel ill."

Grandmother says that _____ doesn't want to go to church today because _____ feels ill.

Football coach: "You needn't worry about sitting on the bench during the next match. We need you for the match!"

My football coach tells _____ that _____ needn't worry about sitting on the bench during the next match because _____ need _____ to play.

Testen

2 Die indirekte Rede

Aufgabe 9 Nimm deine Lösungssätze von Aufgabe 8 und setze sie in die Vergangenheit, indem du jeweils das einleitende Verb in die Vergangenheit setzt.

Jasper said that he had met a wonderful girl and that he felt very happy.

Aufgabe 10 Unterstreiche die richtige Verbform.

Hannah: "School starts at 9:00 a.m. in Great Britain."
Hannah says that school started / starts / had started at 9:00 a.m. in Great Britain.
Sean: "I haven't seen my girlfriend for a week now because she has got the flu."
Sean said that he has not seen / is not seeing / hadn't seen his girlfriend for a week because she has / had got / is having the flu.
The children: "We hadn't finished our maths test when the fire alarm went off."
The children said that they hadn't had finished / hadn't finished / didn't finish their maths test when the fire alarm went off.

Aufgabe 11 Übersetze. Schreibe in dein Übungsheft.

Die Lehrerin sagte den Schülern, dass sie mit dem Ergebnis der Klassenarbeit sehr zufrieden sei.

Mila fragte Paula, ob sie schon den neuen Film mit Jennifer Lawrence gesehen habe.

Die Mutter bat den Sohn, die Musik leiser zu stellen.

Sie sagte, dass sie von dem großen Lärm Kopfschmerzen habe.

Testen

2 Die indirekte Rede

Klassenarbeit 3 — 45 Minuten

Aufgabe 12

Auch Modalverben müssen in der indirekten Rede verändert werden. Gib den richtigen Ersatz an.

can ⇨ _____   shall ⇨ _____

must ⇨ _____   may ⇨ _____

Aufgabe 13

Wandle die Sätze in die indirekte Rede um. Verwende dabei **reporting verbs** in der Vergangenheit.

Teacher to pupils: "Be quiet! You mustn't talk during the lesson!"

_____

Zoe to her sister: "You need to take care of our horse while we'll be in London next week."

_____

Tom to the driver: "Go down Main Street and turn right at the first traffic lights."

_____

Teacher: "Don't forget to study your vocabulary!"

_____

Aufgabe 14

Lillys Tante ist mit ihrer Familie nach Neuseeland ausgewandert, und Lilly unterhält sich am Computer über Skype mit ihrem Cousin. Der gleichaltrige Samuel berichtet seiner Cousine vom Schulalltag am anderen Ende der Welt.

> Imagine, I can sleep in every day. School starts at 9 a.m. only. And we have very different subjects over here: on Mondays, for example, we have a subject called "Taha Maori", which means that we discuss the Maori, who are the native **(eingeboren)** people over here, side of a question. On Thursdays, we have home economics, where we bake bread, make muffins and learn to cook. And we don't go home for lunch: Every student stays at least till 3:30 p.m. But school is cool over here: the teachers have a different way of teaching, we do a lot of project work, and it never gets boring. Why don't you visit me soon?

Testen

2 Die indirekte Rede

Now Lilly tells her mother: "Mum, Samuel has invited me to New Zealand! He said that I should visit him soon. And he told me about his school: …

_____
_____
_____
_____
_____
_____
_____
_____
_____
_____
_____ "

Aufgabe 15 ⋆⋆ Setze die folgenden Sätze in die indirekte Rede. Suche dir dazu aus dem Wortkasten das passende einleitende Verb. Setze die Verben immer ins **past tense**.

to want to know – to tell (2x) – to ask – to say – to warn

Ben to the kids: "Please don't make so much noise."
_____

Newspaper reporter: "Did you see how the accident happened?"
_____

Mother to son: "Did you get the job?"
_____

Teacher to class: "The train to London leaves the station at 9 a.m. Be there on time, we won't wait for latecomers!"
_____

Father to son: "Here are the keys for my car. But be careful!"
_____

Testen

2 Die indirekte Rede

Aufgabe 16

 Du hast heute Maya getroffen. Sie hat dir erzählt, was ihr gestern Morgen passiert ist. Lies den Text und schreibe dann eine E-Mail, in der du deiner Freundin Emily erzählst, was Maya dir erzählt hat.

> "Me and my friend Aisha arrived at the bus station this morning, when we noticed a strange man across the street. He seemed to be waiting for somebody. Suddenly, another man on a bike cycled along and stopped. We could see that the two men exchanged an envelope before they parted in different directions.
> A few minutes later a police car arrived and stopped at the bus stop. Constable Miller told us that the police were tracking some drug dealers and he wanted to know whether we had seen something."

Dear Emily,
Maya told me today …

Wissen

3 Relativsätze

3.1 Notwendige und nicht notwendige Relativsätze

Relativsätze werden durch ein Relativpronomen *(who, which, that, whose)* eingeleitet: ○ *who* wird für **Personen** verwendet, ○ *which* steht bei **Dingen.**	This is the girl **who/that** lost her exercise book.
Sowohl *who* als auch *which* können durch *that* ersetzt werden.	We have a car **which/that** is big enough to seat seven people.
Whose kann sowohl bei Personen als auch bei Dingen stehen. Es drückt eine Zugehörigkeit oder einen Besitz aus.	That's the girl **whose mother** won the song contest last year.
Zum Prädikat des Relativsatzes gehörende **Präpositionen** stehen in der Regel **nach** dem Vollverb.	The woman **who** I was **talking to** is Hanna's mother.
Aufgepasst: Steht die Präposition vor dem Relativsatz, wird *who* zu *whom*.	The woman **to whom** I was **talking** is Hanna's mother.
Relativsätze, die man nicht weglassen kann, ohne dass der Satz seinen Sinn verliert, heißen **notwendige Relativsätze** *(defining relative clauses)*. Es steht kein Komma und das Relativpronomen darf nicht weggelassen werden.	He was the man who saved my life. It was my best friend who gave me that wonderful present.
Stehen im Relativsatz Informationen, die weggelassen werden können, ohne dass sich dadurch die Aussage des Hauptsatzes ändert, handelt es sich um **nicht notwendige Relativsätze** *(non-defining relative clauses)*. Das Komma muss stehen.	Lea's sisters, who are ten and seven years old, are both able to play an instrument. The book, which I am reading at the moment, is very interesting.
Ist das Relativpronomen das Objekt eines notwendigen Relativsatzes, kann es weggelassen werden. Solche Relativsätze nennt man **contact clauses.**	The trip **that** we took to San Francisco was very interesting. = The trip we took to San Francisco was very interesting.

Üben

3 Relativsätze

Übung 1

 Unterstreiche die Relativpronomen im folgenden Text.

Lisa's mum, who usually is a wonderful woman, hears strange voices from Lisa's room. She knocks at her daughter's door, which is not only closed, but locked.

Mum: "Lisa, who else is in there besides you? Whose voices do I hear?"

Lisa: "Well … well … I'm listening to the radio!"

Mum: "Who is that singer, then?"

Lisa: "She's the one who just became popular this year. I've forgotten her name."

Mum: "I see … listen, can I borrow that scarf that you bought yesterday."

Lisa: "Err, yes … well, Mum – come on in! Look, that's Mason. He is the one who is new to our class."

Mum: "Hello Mason! Nice to meet you!"

Mason: "Nice to meet you, too."

Übung 2

 Ergänze Relativpronomen und Verb. Achte dabei besonders auf die Stellung der zum Verb gehörigen Präposition!

The school _____ I _____ (to go to) is just around the corner.

The girl _____ my daughter _____ just _____ (to talk to) is very beautiful.

The album _____ the children _____ (to listen to) at the moment has just been released.

The job _____ I _____ (to apply for) last year was very well paid.

The teacher _____ _____ (to talk about) his last school trip for over an hour teaches English at the local grammar school.

The people _____ I _____ (to work with) promised to throw a birthday party for me.

187

Üben

3 Relativsätze

Übung 3

 Wähle aus dem grünen und roten Kasten je einen Satz aus und verbinde sie mit einem passenden Relativpronomen.

Rot:
- My best friend can't go to the party tonight.
- Our family cannot afford a bigger house.
- My friend Amy had her second baby in February, too.
- The post office is opposite the shopping mall.
- The book is very interesting.
- My father takes my mother out to dinner every Sunday.
- My sister has got a lot of nice dresses.
- The seal was very big.

Grün:
- We are no millionaires.
- I got it for my birthday.
- She likes to dance.
- She lent me a very nice dress for the ball tonight.
- He is almost eighty years now.
- It sells stamps and all kinds of stationary.
- We gave it some fish.
- Her sister had her first baby in February.

Üben

3 Relativsätze

Übung 4

Füge die richtigen Relativpronomen ein. Vergiss nicht, dort Kommas zu setzen, wo diese nötig sind.

The actress _____ had been ill for some months looked very tired yesterday.

Is that the photo _____ they were talking about?

My grandmother _____ lives in Los Angeles always sends me presents for my birthday and for Christmas.

Is this the book _____ you were looking for?

Lily _____ two sisters also play an instrument is just practising the cello.

Is it you _____ essay the teacher read aloud?

Germany is not the only country _____ has a good football team.

This is the new car _____ I told you about.

The reporter wanted to talk to the woman _____ had saved the baby.

Übung 5

Übersetze.

Das Haus, das blaue Türen hat, ist sehr groß.

_____

Autofahrer, die viel Alkohol trinken, können sehr gefährlich sein.

_____

Ich habe das Mädchen, deren Schwester Emma heißt, gestern in der Bücherei gesehen.

_____

_____

Der Junge, der so gut Fußball spielen kann, hat sich das Bein gebrochen.

_____

Sie las ein Buch, das ihre Freunde ihr empfohlen hatten.

_____

Testen

3 Relativsätze

Klassenarbeit  45 Minuten

Aufgabe 1 ★

Setze das fehlende Relativpronomen ein. Achte darauf, ob es sich um eine Sache oder eine Person handelt! Entscheide auch, ob du das Relativpronomen **that** in den folgenden Beispielen wählen kannst.

Jamil is going to the cinema with the girl _____ lives next door.

I know the girl _____ father was in the accident last night.

Where's the newspaper _____ was lying on the sofa?

That's the man _____ I told you about.

Do you like people _____ like to show off *(angeben)*?

My sister has got a job _____ she really enjoys.

Is that the family _____ dog always sleeps in our garden?

Aufgabe 2 ★★

Verbinde die Sätze mithilfe eines passenden Relativpronomens. Setze Kommata, wo es notwendig ist.

The girls have been to a pop concert. It was in Berlin.
_____

My three daughters are very tired. They will have to go to bed soon.
_____

Maya lives in San Francisco. She was born there.
_____

Annie gave me a book. She had got it from her father before.
_____

Tim is an author. He writes fictional books.
_____

Deniz sent me an invitation for her birthday party. I will accept it.
_____

Testen

3 Relativsätze

Aufgabe 3

Trage das richtige Relativpronomen ein. Achtung: Manchmal gibt es zwei Möglichkeiten! Setze Kommata, wo nötig.

Once every ten years, the school choir of a local High School performs Carl Orff's *Carmina Burana*. It is a well-known song arrangement _____ is known worldwide. One time, Carl Orff _____ is the composer even came to the school to watch. The photos _____ were taken at that time reappeared in the local newspaper recently.

All the children _____ are members of the choir will have to wear the same T-shirt. The art classes _____ did all the required stage decorations also designed a programme. All the three performances _____ will be held at the school auditorium are sold out already.

Aufgabe 4

Nur eine Antwort stimmt. Kreuze an.

- London, ☐ when ☐ that ☐ where my grandmother works, is a very expensive city.
- This is the woman ☐ which ☐ who ☐ whose won the trip to Paris.
- I met this girl yesterday ☐ who ☐ whose ☐ whom boyfriend is in my daughter's class.
- The school ☐ which ☐ where ☐ who I go to is a public school.
- Lisa, ☐ who ☐ which ☐ who's lives next door, is a very lively *(lebhaft)* girl.
- The White House, ☐ which ☐ who ☐ whom is the residence of the president of United States, is in Washington D.C.
- I dropped the book ☐ where ☐ that ☐ when I like most in the river while reading it on a boat.

Testen

3 Relativsätze

Aufgabe 5

Erstelle eigene Sätze. Vergiss das Relativpronomen nicht.

difficult / play / music / everyone / enjoys

_____

my sister / likes / rock music / not like / folk songs

_____

our friend / plays / the bass guitar / give / a concert / next Friday

_____

met a woman / I / can speak six languages

_____

has stolen / I / bought / my red bike / last year / somebody

_____

very friendly / work in that office / not are / the people

_____

Aufgabe 6

 Verbessere die Sätze, indem du das falsche Relativpronomen durchstreichst und den Satz richtig aufschreibst.

Beispiel: That's the school ~~to that~~ I go. ⇨ **That's the school that I go to.**

Is that the girl who's photo was in the papers yesterday?

_____

That's the hotel at whose we stayed.

_____

Where is the lady which lost her purse?

_____

Where is the pen with that I always write?

_____

That's the boy who sister is good at French.

_____

Wissen

4 Satzverkürzungen

4.1 Satzverkürzungen mit Gerundium

Das Gerundium *(gerund)* wird gebildet, indem man an den Infinitiv des Vollverbs ein *-ing* anhängt.	to be ⇨ be**ing**, to go ⇨ go**ing**, to talk ⇨ talk**ing**, to die ⇨ dy**ing**, to love ⇨ lov**ing**
Wie den Infinitiv gibt es das Gerundium ◦ im Präsens Aktiv und Passiv, ◦ im Perfekt Aktiv und Passiv.	loving – being loved, having loved – having been loved
Im Satz wird das Gerundium ähnlich wie das Substantiv verwendet. Es kann ◦ als **Subjekt** oder ◦ als **Objekt** eines Satzes auftreten.	**Swimming** („wer oder was?" ⇨ *Subjekt*) is a lot of fun. I like **eating** („wen oder was?" ⇨ *Objekt*) ice cream in summer.

Das Gerundium nach Verben

Zahlreiche Verben erfordern den Gebrauch des Gerundiums als Objekt. Dazu gehören:

to admit	*to imagine*	Anna enjoys hiking in the Alps.
to avoid	*to keep*	My mother suggests going for a walk.
to consider	*to like*	They have discussed raising their baby
to defend	*to mind*	bilingually.
to delay	*to miss*	She dislikes getting up early.
to deny	*to need*	I don't mind sleeping outside at all.
to detest	*to practise*	
to discuss	*to resist*	
to dislike	*to stop*	
to enjoy	*to suggest*	
to excuse	*to understand*	
to finish		

Achtung: Nach den Verben *to begin, to bother, to continue, to hate, to intend, to love, to start* kann sowohl das Gerundium als auch der Infinitiv stehen. Die Bedeutung verändert sich nicht.

Chris **continued working** in London. *Oder:* Chris **continued to work** in London.
He **loves living** in the city. *Oder:* He **loves to live** in the city.

Wissen

4 Satzverkürzungen

Auch einige Verben, die fest mit einer **Präposition** verbunden sind, erzwingen den Gebrauch des Gerundiums:

to agree with	*to feel like*	I apologize for being late.
to apologize for	*to give up*	The pupils concentrate on reading the text.
to complain about / of	*to insist on*	It's so hot. I feel like eating another ice cream.
to concentrate on	*to keep on*	We are looking forward to seeing you again next summer.
to cope with	*to look forward to*	My father has been talking about moving for five years now.
to decide against	*to succeed in*	
to depend on	*to take part in*	
to die of	*to talk about / of*	
to dream about / of	*to think of*	

Das gilt auch, wenn ein Objekt zwischen Verb und Präposition steht.

The police officer accused him of having ignored the red light.

Das Gerundium nach Substantiven

Das Gerundium folgt auf bestimmte **Substantive,** wenn sie mit einer **Präposition** verwendet werden, etwa:

alternative to, interest in, chance of, invitation to, danger of, method of, demand for, possibility of, dislike for / of, problem of, doubt about, reason for, experience in, trouble in

They don't have an alternative to driving a van, they need the many seats.
They have a chance of winning the lottery.
She has a lot of experience in teaching.
There is a reason for watering the plants in summer.

Merke: Auch nach **Präpositionen** allein kann das Gerundium stehen:

after, before, by, for, instead of, on, without

After eating lunch she did her homework.
Instead of watching TV you'd better read a book.

Auch in bestimmten **Redewendungen** steht das Gerundium. Dazu gehören:

can't stand – can't help – it's no use – it's no good – to be busy – to be worth – to spend / to waste time – How about …?

He spent a lot of time trying to find a birthday present for his girlfriend.
It's not worth reading this book.
How about going out for dinner tonight?

Üben

4 Satzverkürzungen

Übung 1

 Die folgenden sechs Verbverbindungen erfordern das Gerundium. Übersetze und trage die Verbindungen in das Kreuzworträtsel ein.

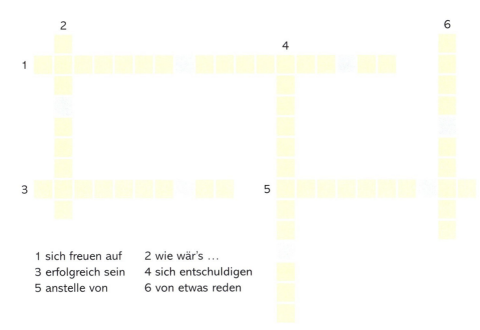

1 sich freuen auf 2 wie wär's …
3 erfolgreich sein 4 sich entschuldigen
5 anstelle von 6 von etwas reden

Übung 2

 Vervollständige die Sätze mithilfe des Gerundiums.

Dilek dreams of _____ (to become) a photographer.

We are looking forward to _____ (to see) you again in San Francisco next summer.

He apologizes for _____ (to be) late.

They are considering _____ away to a different area because of crime.

The school delays _____ (to open) the new sports hall.

Are you proud of _____ (to win) the competition?

I dislike _____ (to go) to the zoo with my family.

When I moved school, I missed _____ (to learn) with my old classmates.

Üben

4 Satzverkürzungen

Übung 3

 Verbinde die Sätze mithilfe des Gerundiums.

My sister stays out late every Saturday night. She enjoys it.
 My sister enjoys staying out late every Saturday night.

My brother sews *(nähen)* his own clothes. He is good at it.
___

My father always reads many stories aloud to his grandchildren. They like it.
___

Sadie might become a movie star one day. Her boyfriend doesn't even like the idea of it.
___
___

Olivia wants to move out when she's 18. She is talking of it already.
___

Rico spends a lot of money on books. His mum is very fond of it.
___

Samuel has to go to the dentist's again. He is frightened of it.
___
___

Übung 4

 Richtig oder falsch?

	true	false
How about travelling to Spain next week?	☐	☐
He spent a lot of time to try to find a birthday present for his mum.	☐	☐
She has no trouble reading one hundred pages per day.	☐	☐
After to eat dinner they enjoyed a movie.	☐	☐
Your pizza is so delicious. I feel like eating another piece of it.	☐	☐
I agree to go by car.	☐	☐

Üben

4 Satzverkürzungen

 Übersetze und verwende das Gerundium.

Übung 5

Wie wär's, wenn wir heute Nachmittag Eis essen gehen?
_____
_____

Ich habe keine Schwierigkeiten Englisch zu lernen.
_____

Interessierst du dich dafür, Fußball zu spielen?
_____

Denkst du darüber nach, dir einen neuen Computer zu kaufen?
_____
_____

Manche Mädchen träumen davon, Pilotin zu werden.
_____
_____

Sie hat eine Menge Erfahrung im Unterrichten.
_____

Wissen

4 Satzverkürzungen

4.2 Satzverkürzungen mit Infinitivkonstruktionen

Im Englischen lässt sich mithilfe einer Infinitivkonstruktion manches verkürzter ausdrücken, als es im Deutschen möglich ist.	My mother **wanted me to help** her shop. ⇨ *Meine Mutter **wollte, dass** ich ihr beim Einkaufen **helfe**.*
Infinitive können in solchen verkürzten Sätzen entweder mit *to* oder ohne *to* stehen.	My mother allowed me **to stay** out late. I saw my friend **cross** the street.
Nach Verben des Denkens, Wünschens, Aufforderns, Veranlassens und Verursachens steht nach Verb und direktem Objekt ein Infinitiv mit *to*. Dazu gehören: *to advise, to ask, to believe, to consider, to encourage, to expect, to force, to imagine, to order, to permit, to persuade, to teach, to tell, to warn*	They don't allow their daughters to stay out late. She wants him to put the baby to sleep. The teacher advised the pupils to read the book. The police permitted the crowd to watch the space rocket take off.
Ein Infinitiv mit *to* steht auch ◦ nach Adjektiven des Gefühlsausdrucks, ◦ nach *right, wrong, easy, hard, difficult, certain, welcome* sowie ◦ nach Superlativen oder Zahlwörtern.	They were delighted to hear about the newborn baby. It was wrong to leave the children alone. In my opinion, Frank is the best singer to play at the charity concert.
Mit einem Infinitiv kann man auch einen Fragesatz verkürzen.	I wondered what I should say to him. ⇨ I wondered what to say to him.
Merke: Manche Verben können entweder mit einem Gerundium (↗ Kap. 4.1) oder einer Infinitivkonstruktion stehen: *to begin, to bother, to continue, to hate, to intend, to love, to start* Die Bedeutung ist in beiden Fällen gleich.	Amy **continued working** after she had the baby. = Amy **continued to work** after she had the baby. My mother **loves living** close to her grandchildren. = My mother **loves to live** close to her grandchildren.

Üben

4 Satzverkürzungen

Wissen+

Ausdruck eines Zwecks

Der Infinitiv mit *to* kann nach *in order to* stehen, wenn ein Zweck zum Ausdruck gebracht werden soll.

She opened the window in order to let some fresh air in.

Übung 6

Formuliere vollständige Sätze. Verwende dabei eine Infinitivkonstruktion.

the mother / play the piano / her daughter / encourage

_____

the parents / instead of dinner / not allow / their children / eat chocolate

_____

study hard / the students / to be advised

_____

Linnea / wear / for the concert / what / cannot decide

_____

be easy / find / it / your place

_____

Übung 7

Gerundium oder Infinitiv? Höre dir Track 3 an und ergänze die Verbform.

I can't stand _____ the bathroom.

Grandfather loves _____ for a walk.

It is right _____ the bathroom every second day.

It's not worth _____ lottery tickets. Most tickets never win.

They were delighted _____ that they had won the lottery.

How about _____ for a walk?

Üben

4 Satzverkürzungen

Übung 8 ⭐⭐ Verbinde passende Satzteile. Es gibt mehr Satzenden, als du benötigst.

- It is hard
- My parents taught
- Children are expected
- Tarek allowed his friend
- My uncle couldn't persuade his family

- me to forget his keys.
- to buy him a new bike.
- to hurry home after the accident.
- to get up every morning at 5 o'clock.
- to send him to a private school as a child.
- me to always be on time.
- to help their brothers and sisters.

Übung 9 ⭐⭐⭐ Übersetze. Schreibe in dein Übungsheft.

Die Polizei zwang sie, ihr die Waffe zu geben.

Sie rieten ihm weniger Energie zu verbrauchen.

Ich warne dich, nicht zu häufig Süßigkeiten zu essen.

Pat fährt in den Urlaub nach Frankreich, um ihr Französisch zu verbessern.

Übung 10 ⭐⭐⭐ Steht im folgenden Dialog jeweils ein Gerundium, ein Infinitiv oder ist beides möglich? Unterstreiche, was richtig ist.

Gerald: "I was thinking of finding / to find ways to save the planet with our actions. Do you have any ideas?"

Asha: "If we continue to waste / wasting so much energy, I don't see how we could protect the environment."

Gerald: "Why don't we take part in discussing / to discuss this subject in our school club? It starts after the break."

Asha: "Do you expect me to come / coming with you today? I'd hate to go / going there today because it's my mum's birthday."

Gerald: "Okay. You are welcome to join / joining me but I won't insist on you to come / coming along today. I'm going to tell you all about it tomorrow in the bus."

Asha: "Great. I'm looking forward to listen / listening to your report. See you!"

Wissen

4 Satzverkürzungen

4.3 Satzverkürzungen mit Partizipialkonstruktionen

Das **Partizip Präsens** *(present participle)* wird durch Anhängen von *-ing* gebildet. Es wird immer aktivisch verwendet und steht ○ nach einem Substantiv, um einen Relativsatz zu ersetzen, ○ vor einem Substantiv und hat dann die Funktion eines Adjektivs.	to walk ⇨ walking, to sing ⇨ singing The girl **playing football** (= who plays football) is my younger sister Lily. a **living** legend
Das *present participle* folgt auf ○ Verben der Wahrnehmung: *to look, to notice, to see, to hear, to feel, to smell,* ○ Verben der Ruhe und Bewegung: *to lie, to sit, to stand, to come, to walk.*	She saw him kissing another woman. The girls stood talking about their homework.
Das **Partizip Perfekt** *(past participle)* wird durch Anhängen von *-ed* oder unregelmäßig (↗ Band 7, Kap. 4.2) gebildet. Es wird immer passivisch verwendet und steht ○ vor einem Substantiv, um einen Relativsatz zu ersetzen, ○ nach einem Substantiv, um einen Relativsatz zu ersetzen, wenn das *past participle* selbst durch eine (adverbiale) Bestimmung der Zeit oder des Ortes erweitert wird.	to talk ⇨ talked, to buy ⇨ bought The newly **built school** was opened last week. (*Statt:* The school that was newly built was opened last week.) The **school built near Park Lane** was opened last week. (*Statt:* The school that was built near Park Lane was opened last week.)
Adverbialsätze (↗ Band 7, Kap. 7.1) können durch Partizipialkonstruktionen ersetzt werden, wenn das Subjekt des Hauptsatzes mit dem Subjekt des Nebensatzes identisch ist. Dazu gehören: ○ Adverbialsätze der Zeit, die mit *when* oder *while* eingeleitet werden, ○ Adverbialsätze des Grundes, die mit *as, because* oder *since* eingeleitet werden.	**When she heard that** her grandma was at the door, the little girl ran to greet her. ⇨ **Hearing** that her grandma was … **Because he was thirsty,** he went to a shop to buy some juice. ⇨ **Being thirsty** he went to a shop …

Üben

4 Satzverkürzungen

Übung 11

 Verkürze die Sätze mithilfe einer Partizipialkonstruktion.

The boy who plays football is dreaming of a big career.

___

The swimming pool that was built in our backyard wasn't worth its money.

___

Chloe knows the boy who lives next door very well.

___

Because I was reading an interesting book, I did not answer the phone.

___

Wissen⁺

Verben mit Gerundium und Infinitiv

Einige Verben können mit Infinitiv oder Gerundium stehen (↗ Kap. 4.1). Je nach Gebrauch verändert sich in einigen Fällen die Bedeutung.

to remember (to forget) to do sth. – (nicht) daran denken, etw. zu tun	I must **remember (mustn't forget) to buy** some milk today.
to remember (to forget) doing sth. – sich (nicht) daran erinnern, etw. getan zu haben	I **remember (forgot) buying** that book.
to stop to do sth. = anhalten, um etw. zu tun	He **stopped** his car **to save** the hedgehog *(Igel)*.
to stop doing sth. = damit aufhören, etw. zu tun	He **stopped smoking** a year ago.
to go on to do sth. = dazu übergehen, etw. anderes zu tun	First, she spoke French to her son. Then she **went on to speak** English to her guests.
to go on doing sth. = damit weitermachen, etw. zu tun	She **went on speaking** French although everybody at the party would have preferred an English conversation.

Üben

4 Satzverkürzungen

Übung 12

Welche Übersetzung ist richtig? Kreuze an.

Ich muss daran denken, das Buch zu kaufen.
- [ ] I must remember to buy the book.
- [ ] I must remember buying the book.

Meine Tochter hat aufgehört zu rauchen.
- [ ] My daughter stopped to smoke.
- [ ] My daughter stopped smoking.

Wir versuchten den Weg aus dem Wald zu finden.
- [ ] We tried to find our way out of the forest.
- [ ] We tried finding our way out of the forest.

Ich schlage doch gar nicht vor, dass wir in den Ferien zuhause bleiben!
- [ ] I'm not suggesting staying at home during the holidays!
- [ ] I'm not suggesting to stay at home during the holidays!

Hast du nicht bemerkt, dass ich ein Tor geschossen habe?
- [ ] Didn't you notice me scoring a goal?
- [ ] Didn't you notice me to score a goal?

Übung 13

Ergänze die Sätze mit einer Partizipialkonstruktion.

The mountain biker _overtook the hiker climbing_ up the hills. (overtook – hiker – climb)

I knew it couldn't be true as soon as I _____ _____ at her sister. (noticed – my girlfriend – smile)

I was driving a lonely road when I _____ _____ into the nearby forest. (heard – something – crash)

I am fed up with waiting for dinner at this silly restaurant. – Oh, look! I think I can _____ to our table.
(see – the waiter – come up)

Üben

4 Satzverkürzungen

Übung 14

 Ändere die rot hervorgehobenen Verben zu einer Partizipialkonstruktion.

Beispiel: When Maya and Sofia came into the ice cream parlour, one of the boys working there noticed them. ⇨ **One of the boys working there noticed Maya and Sofia coming into the ice cream parlour.**

A few minutes later he passed by their table as he walked over to a nearby couple to take their orders. While he took the couple's order, he noticed that Maya whispered something to her friend. From where he was standing, he could hear her as she talked excitedly to Sofia and asked her whether she had noticed him. And when the boy took the girls' order, he noticed that he had met the girls before and that he could now start a conversation very easily.

_____
_____
_____
_____
_____
_____
_____
_____
_____
_____

Übung 15

 Übersetze.

Stimmt es, dass du schlecht beim Schwimmen bist?
_____

Mein Bruder interessiert sich nicht für die Schule.
_____

Die Lehrerin ermutigt ihre Schülerinnen Mathematik zu studieren.
_____
_____

Was hältst du von Menschen, die überall hin mit dem Auto fahren?
_____
_____

Testen

4 Satzverkürzungen

Klassenarbeit 60 Minuten

Aufgabe 1

 Welches Wort passt nicht in die Reihe? Streiche es durch.

seen – heard – read – love

played – talked – written – kissed

go – drawn – got – kept

paying – singing – told – writing

Aufgabe 2

* Setze die zum Gerundium gehörende passende Präposition ein.

She has a lot of experience _____ dancing.

Bo has a good method _____ learning.

Father has a reason _____ asking me twice about my results in the last maths exam.

They have a chance _____ winning the championship.

Instead _____ watching TV you'd better go jogging.

Aufgabe 3

 Schreibe sinnvolle Sätze. Verwende das Gerundium.

I enjoy	eat out	historic novels
I dislike	listen to	on Sundays
I hate	read	loud music
I don't like	play	the piano

_____
_____
_____
_____
_____

Testen

4 Satzverkürzungen

Aufgabe 4

Infinitiv oder Gerundium?

This text is easy _____ (to read).

Remember _____ (to pick up) the mail on your way home.

We all look forward to _____ (to see) you again next summer.

Mother expects me _____ (to pass) the driving test.

_____ (to run) is a lot of fun.

Phil denied (!) _____ (to eat) all of the candy.

Aufgabe 5

Schreibe ganze Sätze. Verwende dabei eine Infinitivkonstruktion.

Mia / want / be / a movie star

_____

The parents / not allow / the children / watch TV / the whole day

_____

Yesterday / my friend / convince / me / visit / the museum

_____

The doctor / warn / his patient / gain weight

_____

Aufgabe 6

Verben mit oder ohne Infinitiv und Bedeutungsänderungen. Nur eine Übersetzung ist richtig. Welche?

Er hat schon wieder vergessen anzuhalten, um Brot einzukaufen.
☐ Once again he forgot to stop to buy some bread.
☐ Once again he forgot to stop buying some bread.

Ich erinnere mich gut daran, wie wir im letzten Jahr in einem langen Stau stecken geblieben sind.
☐ I very well remember getting stuck in a bad traffic jam last summer.
☐ I very well remember to get stuck in a bad traffic jam last summer.

Sie hörte auf auszugehen, nachdem ihre Mutter gestorben war.
☐ She stopped to go out after her mother had died.
☐ She stopped going out after her mother had died.

Testen

4 Satzverkürzungen

Aufgabe 7

Infinitiv oder Gerundium? Setze die richtige Verbform ein.

On our trip to Santa Cruz, we stopped _____ (to have) a cup of coffee.

Would you mind _____ (to turn) down the air conditioning, please? My eyes are watering.

Did you remember _____ (to switch off) the heater before you left the house?

Would you please stop _____ (to talk)?

I would love _____ (to work) at home.

Aufgabe 8

Verkürze die Sätze mithilfe einer Partizipialkonstruktion.

When we arrived at home, we were welcomed by my mother with a home-cooked meal.

_____

As he realized how late it was, Sam decided not to phone his friend.

_____

My mother, who had worked worked in London when she was young, had picked up her English there.

_____

Aufgabe 9

Übersetze und schreibe in dein Übungsheft.

Es hat keinen Sinn, sich über Hausaufgaben zu beschweren.

Es war falsch, die Kinder alleine ins Kino zu schicken.

Du solltest jetzt Hausaufgaben machen, anstatt Fernsehen zu schauen.

Mein Vater erlaubte mir, auf die Party zu gehen.

Bitte vergiss nicht, deine Schuhe zu putzen.

Er hat vergangenes Jahr aufgehört, Tennis zu spielen.

Wissen

5 Texte lesen und verstehen

5.1 Sachtexte

Ein englischer Text gleicht im Aufbau einem deutschen Text. Grundsätzlich sind zu unterscheiden:
- Sachtexte *(non-fictional texts)* und
- literarische Texte *(fictional texts)*.

Sachtexte: Artikel in Zeitungen und Zeitschriften, Sachbücher, wissenschaftliche Texte, (Wahl)reden …
Literarische Texte: Gedichte, Erzählungen, Kurzgeschichten, Dramen, Romane, Kinder- und Jugendliteratur

Sachtexte vermitteln Informationen und erklären Sachverhalte. Sie haben daher stets einen Bezug zur erfahrbaren Wirklichkeit. Um solche Texte besser zu verstehen, gehst du am besten schrittweise vor:
- **Lies** den Text ein erstes Mal in seiner Gesamtheit **gründlich** durch.
- Löse die **Abkürzungen** auf, die im Text vorkommen!

Tipp: Jedes Wörterbuch hat ein Abkürzungsverzeichnis.

i. e. = id est (lat.) = *das heißt / das ist*
e. g. = example given = *zum Beispiel*

- Schlage **unbekannte Wörter** und Begriffe oder Redewendungen nach. Versuche dabei, dich auf die wichtigen Begriffe zu konzentrieren – so manches Wort kannst du dir auch aus dem Zusammenhang erschließen!

If you get seriously injured, you'll better go to hospital. But if you only graze your knee, a plaster is a good cure. (to graze one's knee ⇨ *die Knie aufschürfen*)

- Achte beim Lesen auf sogenannte **Schlüsselbegriffe** *(keywords):* Unterstreiche wesentliche Textstellen und Schlagwörter.

Tipp: Arbeite mit verschiedenen Farben.

Shakespeare's play *Romeo and Juliet* is a classical **love story.** Romeo Montague and Juliet Capulet are teenagers who fall in love but their families are bitter enemies. They marry in secret but in the end, their actions end in tragedy.

Ergänzen Grafiken, Fotos, Diagramme, Tabellen, Landkarten oder Ähnliches den Text, musst du genau zuordnen können, auf welche Textstelle sich die zusätzlichen Informationen beziehen.

5 Texte lesen und verstehen

Üben

Übung 1

Read these lines.

> At the beginning of the last century, moving pictures were invented. At first, these pictures were recorded without sound. In a movie of today, however, sound effects and music are as important as the story itself.
>
> Modern movies also use a lot of special effects to attract publicity. And, of course, actors and actresses are very important. Famous movie stars earn a lot of money and often live in a world of their own.

Übung 2

Which of the following headlines does match the text above?

☐ An unreal world

☐ Stars in the universe

☐ A short history of movies

Übung 3

Read the text.

> Many teenagers have a dream of becoming a movie star. Actor Freddie Highmore, from London, was only 13 years old when he became famous. At that time he had been in eight movies, among them the two big projects *Finding Neverland* (*Wenn Träume fliegen lernen,* 2005) and *Charlie and the Chocolate Factory* (*Charlie und die Schokoladenfabrik,* 2005).
>
> Both movies also star Johnny Depp, one of the most famous contemporary actors. Freddie enjoyed working alongside Johnny Depp and thus for Freddie a widespread teenage dream had come true. However, in the following years he did not only star in films but also graduated from school with A grades and earned a degree in Spanish and Arabic at the top university Cambridge in 2014. Later he worked as an intern at a bank in Kuwait. Therefore one cannot be sure that Freddie Highmore is going to make movies for the rest of his life. He's still quite young and that fact gives him enough coolness to state that he's not sure if he wants to make movies for the rest of his life …

Üben

5 Texte lesen und verstehen

Übung 4

 Now answer the following questions to the text in exercise 3.

1. Look again at the list of texts on page 208: Is it a fictional or a non-fictional text?
2. What is the text about?
3. What facts does the text give?
4. What conclusion is drawn at the end?

_____
_____
_____
_____
_____
_____
_____
_____
_____
_____
_____
_____

Wissen+

Auf Englisch nachgefragt!

Die fünf wichtigsten Fragen an einen Text, die sogenannten W-Fragen, lauten:

Who? What? When? Where? Why?

Who reports about what?
Who is involved?
What is the text about?
When does/did the event happen?
Where does the story take place?
Why does something happen?
And/or why is it important to report on?

Üben

5 Texte lesen und verstehen

Übung 5

Something got wrong here.
1. Read the two texts carefully.
2. Match the missing sentences (1–6) to the gaps (A–G).
   There is one more gap than you need.
3. Try to find a headline for each story.

Fox-hunting was one of the most criticized activties in Britain. This "sport" involved chasing a fox with a pack of hounds. **A** When the hunters, who rode on horses, finally caught the fox, it was brutally killed by the dogs. **B** They also said that rural Britain needed the hunt because jobs depended on it. Those who were against the hunt said that it was not needed to limit the number of foxes and they wanted it banned because it was unnecessarily cruel.

C The teddy bear is today so much a part of children's and grown-ups' lives that it is hard to believe it was only invented in 1902. **D** It is named after Theodore "Teddy" Roosevelt (1858–1919), the twenty-sixth president of the United States of America (1901–1909). **E** One day, he visited Mississippi and decided to go out hunting for the day. After several hours, he had not shot anything, when one of his aides discovered a lost bear cub *(Bärenjunges)* wandering through the woods. **F** Roosevelt, however, could not bring himself to shoot the defenceless little bear and ordered it to be set free. Reporters following the President made this incident known all over the country. Clifford Berryman, a cartoonist, drew a cartoon showing the President and the bear cub. **G** These toy bears sold like hot cakes and within a year Michtum founded a toy firm that produced hundreds of thousands of teddy bears.

1. "Teddy" Roosevelt was a keen hunter.
2. Fox-hunting has been forbidden in Britain since 2005.
3. The fox had to flee over the open countryside, as all the foxholes had been blocked before the hunt.
4. He caught it, tied it to a tree and brought the President to this tree to shoot the little bear.
5. Morris Michtum, a toyshop owner, put together some little toy bears using the cartoon as a guide.
6. Those who practised and supported the hunt said that hunting was necessary to keep the number of foxes small.

A   B   C   D   E   F   G

Üben

5 Texte lesen und verstehen

Übung 6

 Now answer the following questions to the text in exercise 5.

1. Was Theodore Roosevelt successful when hunting on his visit to Mississippi?
2. What happened to the fox when it was caught?
3. Why were foxes hunted in Great Britian?
4. Why was the toy bear called teddy bear?
5. What happened to the little bear in the woods?
6. How did people in the United States get to know about this incident with the bear?

Wissen

5 Texte lesen und verstehen

5.2 Texte zusammenfassen

Eine Inhaltsangabe *(summary)* gibt die wesentliche(n) Aussage(n) eines Textes wieder. Sie kommt ohne Wertungen oder persönliche Stellungnahmen aus.

Benutze *present tense*-Formen für Sachtexte.	This newspaper article is about a bad car accident. It **informs** us …
Verwende *present tense*- oder *past tense*-Formen für literarische Texte.	Charles Dickens' novel *Oliver Twist* tells the story of a boy who **grows up** in a children's home *oder* who **grew up** in …
Erwähne nur die Hauptpunkte (W-Fragen, ↗ Kap. 5.1).	car accident: who? ⇨ a car and a truck, what? ⇨ a crash, when? ⇨ in the morning, where? ⇨ near Piccadilly Circus
Verwende keine direkte Rede, sondern nur indirekte Rede. *Achtung:* Schreibe nie wortwörtlich ab!	The text mentions that …, The author argues that …

Um ein *summary* zu schreiben, gehst du schrittweise vor:

- Jede Inhaltsangabe braucht einen einleitenden Satz über das Thema, um das es geht.

  The text by (name of author) deals with …

- Im Hauptteil werden die Hauptfiguren, der Ort und, wenn angegeben, die Zeit der Handlung genannt.

  The story itself takes place …
  The main character in the story is a boy / girl / woman / man called …,

- Die Schlussbetrachtung *(conclusion)* fasst den Schluss des Originaltextes zusammen.

  The author concludes …,
  At last / Finally …

Merke: Im *summary* geht es darum, die Inhalte eines Textes mit deinen eigenen Worten zu formulieren. Lediglich die sogenannten Schlüsselbegriffe *(keywords)* solltest du wörtlich übernehmen!

Text: "These two very old people are the father and mother of Mr Pot. Their names are Grandpa Jim and Grandma Jill." ⇨ *Umformulierung:* "Grandpa Jim and Grandma Jill are Mr Pot's parents."

Für die sprachliche Gestaltung eines *summary* gilt außerdem:
- Ersetze Aufzählungen möglichst durch Oberbegriffe.

  ice cream, chocolate, chewing gum ⇨ candy
  apples, pears, bananas, cherries ⇨ fruit

- Verwende eine abwechslungsreiche Sprache und verzichte auf sprachliche Bilder.

Deine eigene Meinung ist in einem *summary* nicht gefragt!

The text is about / deals with / is written / informs / talks about …

Üben

5 Texte lesen und verstehen

Übung 7

Find a matching group term.

T-shirt – socks – skirt – blouse ⇨ _____

cucumber – carrots – cauliflower – broccoli ⇨ _____

plates – cups – bowls ⇨ _____

basketball – football – cycling – cricket ⇨ _____

house – skyscraper – cottage – castle ⇨ _____

Übung 8

To write about writing – solve the crossword puzzle.

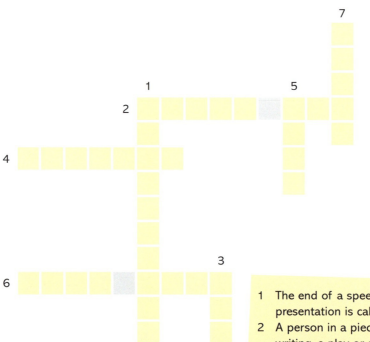

1 The end of a speech or presentation is called …
2 A person in a piece of writing, a play or a movie
3 A person who writes books
4 The place where something happens
5 A form of written words
6 The most important statement in a text can be called the …
7 An (invented) description of events and / or people

Üben

5 Texte lesen und verstehen

Wissen+

Richtig formulieren

Die Hauptaussage *(main idea)* eines Sachtextes gibst du am besten mit Verben des Sagens oder Denkens wieder, z. B. *to introduce, to begin with, to continue, to go on, to argue, to explain, to mention, to point out, to stress, to doubt if, to suggest*

The main subject of the text **is introduced** in line 4 already ...
The author **points out** ...
As a solution, the texts **suggests** ...

Übung 9

 Read the text. After reading it, underline the keywords.

Looking for an answer?

If you're looking for answers, look no further. Our new encyclopedia, the "Encyclopedia 2022", sets new standards:

– 300,000 headwords,
– 40,000 visual elements such as colour photos, charts and diagrams,
– more than 20,000 biographies of important people

fill more than 24,000 pages, so our "Encyclopedia 2022" can be called the biggest encyclopedia ever. With over 125 years of experience and expertise, only the "Encyclopedia 2022" offers its readers an incomparable depth and breadth of various kinds of information. Whether you're up for only a quick access about something that just slipped out of your mind or whether you're interested in detailed articles on almost any imaginable subject, we're here to answer your question!

All entries have been thoroughly revised and updated, and more than 30 % of our articles inform you about new technologies, modern innovations and recent inventions in fields such as nanotechnology and modern genetic research. The 30 volume edition comes with an additional audio-DVD containing high-quality recordings of musical masterpieces, political speeches as well as examples of animal sounds such as the song of the humpback whale etc.

There's almost no information that you won't find in our "Encyclopedia 2022" – don't hesitate: Ensure your own access to first-class, up-to-date knowledge now!

Üben

5 Texte lesen und verstehen

Übung 10

★★★ Now answer the following questions to the text in exercise 9.

1. What kind of text is it?
2. What is the text about?
3. Who is responsible for that text?
4. Where could you read such a text?
5. Why is it written?
6. What do you think: is it an interesting product or not? Give reasons.

_____
_____
_____
_____
_____
_____

Übung 11

★★★ Write a summary.

_____
_____
_____
_____
_____

Übung 12

★★★ Write a short text of five to seven sentences to promote a product or service you would like to sell. Don't forget to think of a slogan too!

_____
_____
_____
_____
_____
_____

Wissen

5 Texte lesen und verstehen

5.3 Literarische Texte

Literarische (erzählende oder fiktionale) Texte gibt es in verschiedenen Formen.	short story – narration – fable – novel – poem – song – drama (comedy, tragedy)
Um einen literarischen Text zu verstehen, beantwortest du zunächst die folgenden Fragen: ○ Wer sind die **Hauptfiguren?** Welche Eigenschaften haben sie? (1) ○ Gibt es **Nebenfiguren?** Welchen Einfluss haben sie auf das Geschehen? (2) ○ **Wo** und **wann** spielt die Handlung? (3) ○ **Was** passiert? (4)	(1) The main character of the story is …, He is quite tall/small, has got vivid eyes … (2) (Name of person) is of minor importance in the story. However, at one point … (3) The story itself takes place in …, The setting of the story is …, The story happens at times when people still went on horseback … (4) The story is about the problem of / the conflict between …, The central event of the story is …
Wenn du einen literarischen Text näher untersuchst, dann solltest du auch die **Charaktere** sowie ihre **Beziehung zueinander** erklären.	The narrator describes (name of person) in detail. She/he is … (Name of person) is introduced at the beginning. She/he is …
Ein wesentliches Kriterium eines literarischen Texts ist seine **Form.** Daher muss immer auch die **sprachliche Gestaltung** beurteilt werden: ○ Wie ist die Handlung erzählt? (1) ○ Wie ist die Wortwahl? (2) ○ Gibt es formale Besonderheiten, die den Text von anderen unterscheiden? (3)	(1) The story begins in the middle of the action. The story has … main part(s). The first part forms the exposition of the story. The narrator (first-person/third-person narrator?) gives a detailed description of … (2) The author uses short sentences/detailed description/few/many words to …, She/he uses slang expressions/formal English/youth language to create authenticity. (3) The story is an example of modern orthography …
Merke: Egal welchen der genannten Punkte du ausführst, ergänze die Aussage immer durch ein **Zitat** aus dem Text!	The author uses slang expressions such as … to describe … (see page …, line(s) …)
Schließlich geht es auch um das **Ende** bzw. den Ausgang der Geschichte: *How does the story end?* oder *What is the author's intention?*	The story shows the reader how …, The story is an example of …, The author wants to show …

Üben

5 Texte lesen und verstehen

Übung 13 The more words you know, the easier it is to write texts of any kind. So brush up your vocabulary. Find the opposite.

expensive ⇔ _____	_____ ⇔ tall
sour ⇔ _____	_____ ⇔ boring
wide ⇔ _____	_____ ⇔ dirty
bright ⇔ _____	_____ ⇔ sad
right ⇔ _____	_____ ⇔ passive

Übung 14 To write about fiction, you need a lot of descriptive adjectives. Cross the odd ones out.

What's a good story like? – A good story is:

> interesting – funny – boring – terrible – thrilling – exciting – comfortable

What are nice people (in "story language": characters) like? – Nice characters are:

> impolite – helpful – polite – furious – loveable – angry – pleasant – stubborn

And mean characters are:

> good-natured – friendly – unfriendly – terrible – bad-tempered – nasty – unpleasant

The atmosphere of a story can be:

> friendly – spooky – familiar – agreeable – pleasant – colourful

Wissen⁺

Englisch? Englisch!
Schon gemerkt? Die Arbeitsanweisungen in diesem Kapitel sind alle auf Englisch! Bestimmt verstehst du trotzdem, was du tun sollst!

Translate. ⇨ *Übersetze!*
Answer the following questions. ⇨ *Beantworte die folgenden Fragen!*
Solve the problem. ⇨ *Löse das Problem!*
In English, please. ⇨ *Auf Englisch, bitte!*

Wissen

5 Texte lesen und verstehen

5.4 Hörverstehen

Richtig zuhören

Achte auf den Rhythmus eines Satzes, um Inhalte leichter und besser zuzuordnen.

falling intonation:
Eine fallende Stimmlage zeigt an, dass ein Gedankengang abgeschlossen ist.

What a fantastic game! ↘
That's such a wonderful bag! ↘

rising intonation:
Eine steigende Stimmlage weist darauf hin, dass dem Sprecher z. B. die Antwort auf eine Frage unklar ist (Yes-/No-questions).

Do you want some more tea? ↗
Are you ready? ↗

emphatic intonation:
Eine auffällige, besondere Betonung verleiht dem betreffenden Wort eine wichtige Bedeutung

Is this **really** your sister?

Inhalte einordnen

Erstens: Die Aufgabenstellung aufmerksam lesen!
Zweitens: Die Textart bestimmen! Egal ob Dialog, wissenschaftlicher Vortrag oder politische Rede – wer die Besonderheiten einer Textart kennt, kann auch die Inhalte schneller erfassen.

You are listening to a dialogue. ⇨ Make a chart *(Tabelle)* and use separate colours, one for each character.

You are listening to some serious information. ⇨ Take down keywords and look them up later.

You are listening to a political speech. ⇨ Sum up the speaker's main idea.

Tipp: Konzentriert zuhören!
Und: Konzentration ist Übungssache (z. B. durch Merkspiele etc.).

Den Ton richtig einordnen

Je nach Gesprächssituation gibt es für dieselbe Aussage unterschiedliche Formulierungen.

formal ⇔ **informal**
to encounter ⇨ to meet

Üben

5 Texte lesen und verstehen

Übung 15

★ What goes where? Listen to track 4 and put the words into the table where they belong.

🎧 4

drinks	fruit and vegetables	containers / wrappings	meals

Übung 16

★★ Two neighbours are talking. Listen to track 5 twice and fill in the gaps.

🎧 5

Jim: "The weather is _____ today, isn't it?"

Lilly: "Do you really think so? I'd say it's rather _____ for May."

Jim: "Well, it's not raining. It _____ all day yesterday. Wasn't that awful?"

Lilly: "I hope it'll be _____ tomorrow. I've bought myself a new skirt that I want to wear."

Jim: "Well, the forecast says that it'll be quite _____ tomorrow, with just a little _____ . So I'm sure you can wear it then."

Übung 17

★★ Listen to track 6 and decide where you can hear the different sentences.

🎧 6

radio news – underground – weather forecast – flight – train station

1. _____
2. _____
3. _____
4. _____
5. _____

Üben

5 Texte lesen und verstehen

Übung 18

7 Listen to track 7. Decide if the sentences are right or wrong and tick the correct box. Write the corrected sentences into your exercise book.

	true	false
You're listening to Radio Rainbow, Germany's most popular radio station.	☐	☐
A postman found an envelope with € 1,000 and took it to the police.	☐	☐
A crazy lover sent off 65 bright pigeons to ask his girlfriend whether she'd marry him.	☐	☐
Manchester United's goalkeeper has just turned down an 8 million Dollar job offer from an American club.	☐	☐

Übung 19

8 Listen to the dialogue from the novel **Women in Love** (track 8) by D.H. Lawrence twice and tick the correct box. Before you do this, read the explanation of some vocabulary from the dialogue and the diffferent options.

to stitch – **sticken** embroidery – **Stickerei**
to reject – **ablehnen** temptation – **Versuchung**

The two sisters Ursula and Gudrun Brangwen are talking about …

☐ love. ☐ marriage. ☐ family experiences.

The two sisters have got different hobbies. Are they doing …

☐ embroidery and reading? ☐ embroidery and drawing?
☐ embroidery and housework?

"A thousand a year, and an awfully nice man." – Ursula is …

☐ exaggerating. ☐ proud about the numbers of men who have been interested in her so far.
☐ showing off.

Who is tempted to get married?

☐ Gudrun ☐ Ursula
☐ both ☐ no one

221

Testen

5 Texte lesen und verstehen

Klassenarbeit 60 Minuten

Aufgabe 1

(*) Write the abbreviations out in full. Then translate the word.

	complete word	German meaning
abbr. ⇨	_____	_____
sing. ⇨	_____	_____
sth ⇨	_____	_____
prep. ⇨	_____	_____
e.g. ⇨	_____	_____
AE ⇨	_____	_____
idm ⇨	_____	_____
sb ⇨	_____	_____

Aufgabe 2

(**) Give definitions.

author: _____

character: _____

theme: _____

fiction: _____

text: _____

Aufgabe 3

(**) Words about writing – Cross the odd ones out.

describe – tell – narrate – fly – report – recount

characterize – portray – identify – desire

story – narration – report – fiction – tale – anecdote

character – figure – type – person – brand

literary – educated – lazy – cultivated – learned

5 Texte lesen und verstehen

Testen

Aufgabe 4

 Read the text and write a summary of no more than fifty words.

The lie detector works on the assumption that people who tell a lie become stressed, and that the stress speeds up their pulse and makes them sweat. These effects can be detected by sensitive instruments. A British scientist found out that a lie detector can be outwitted by meditation techniques such as autogenic training or by imagining to be somewhere else. For this reason lie detectors are heavily criticized. Judges are not allowed to use the results of lie detector tests when passing judgement on the accused at court.

Text by Mathew Barker

Testen

5 Texte lesen und verstehen

Aufgabe 5

Listen to the five texts about some famous English harbours twice (track 9). Then decide if the following statements are true or false and correct the wrong statements.

9

	true	false
Plymouth can be found in Devon.	☐	☐
It is known as a historical place because it was invaded by Drake, Raleigh and Cook.	☐	☐
Mayflower is the name of a very famous ship.	☐	☐
Tenby is an attractive sea resort on the north coast of Wales.	☐	☐
You can go shopping there in lovely shops and walk through narrow streets.	☐	☐
Liverpool is the biggest sea port in Great Britain.	☐	☐
Some dock buildings have been preserved.	☐	☐
Gloucester is famous because of its dome.	☐	☐
The canal in Gloucester, which was opened in 1872, made the city an important inland port.	☐	☐
There is a historic dock complex that can be visited.	☐	☐
Cornwall offers a mild climate for sub-tropical flowers.	☐	☐
Fishing is still a major source of income in Mevagissey.	☐	☐
When it becomes too busy there, the police close the village to motorbikes.	☐	☐

Wissen

6 Englisch sprechen

6.1 Präsentieren

Im Englischunterricht wie später auch im Beruf muss immer wieder präsentiert werden: angefangen von der Vorstellung der eigenen Person bis hin zur Ausarbeitung eines Vortrags zu einem bestimmten Thema. Dabei können verschiedene Medien als Unterstützung eingesetzt werden (z. B. Fotos, Grafiken, Folien *(slides)*, Präsentationsprogramme, Handouts).

Abhängig vom Publikum ist die Sprache eher formell *(formal)* oder informell *(informal)*.	Good morning ladies and gentlemen … (formal) Hi everyone. (informal)
Der Aufbau ist zu einem Teil standardisiert:	
○ Begrüßung,	Good morning. / Hello everyone.
○ ggf. Vorstellung der eigenen Person,	Let me introduce myself. / For those of you who don't know me, my name is …
○ Einführung in das Thema mit Verweis auf die Gliederung / den Aufbau,	My topic today is … / My presentation is about … / The presentation is divided into three parts. First … Then … Finally …
○ ggf. Begründung, warum das Thema für die Zuhörerinnen und Zuhörer wichtig ist,	The topic is important / interesting for you because …
○ thematischer Hauptteil,	
○ kurze Zusammenfassung der wichtigsten Punkte,	So why should you make a trip to New York? Well, first … Second …
○ Dank für das Zuhören,	Thank you for listening.
○ Bitte, Fragen zu stellen (zum Verständnis oder zum Inhalt)	Do you have any questions?
Die Zuhörerinnen und Zuhörer werden dir im Anschluss ein Feedback geben *(peer feedback)*.	I really liked your photos. Your handout was very good but you spoke too quickly. Could you explain …?
Aufgepasst: Schau deine Zuhörerinnen und Zuhörer immer wieder an. Sprech möglichst frei. Verwende daher Karteikarten *(prompt cards)*. Erkläre wichtiges unbekanntes Vokabular auf Englisch.	"detention": You get detention in high school in the US when you are a pupil and break the rules at your school.

Üben

6 Englisch sprechen

Übung 1

* Put the actions into the correct order.

- [ ] Write prompt cards.
- [ ] Tell your listeners how long the presentation will be.
- [ ] Speak clearly and slowly.
- [ ] Practise your presentation.
- [ ] Summarize the main ideas from the texts you read in your own words.
- [ ] Ask for questions.
- [ ] Collect information about your topic on the internet, in newspapers, magazines etc.

Übung 2

* You can use the following phrases to introduce a topic. Draw a line between the phrases with a similar meaning.

Today I'm going to talk about …	I've been interested in this topic as …
My aim is to …	My presentation has four parts.
I hope you will learn a lot about …	Finally, I intend to …
Let me tell you first about the structure …	My topic this morning is …
I was particularly fascinated by this topic because …	I would like to show you that …
At the end I will …	Hopefully my presentation will improve your knowledge about …

Üben

6 Englisch sprechen

Übung 3

 Complete the presentation with words from the box.

> here you can see – first I'd like to tell –
> I'll start by explaining – I'll now move on to –
> I think you will agree – my talk will – now have a look

Hi. Let me introduce myself to you. My name is Amar Patel. I'm 14 years old and I'm from Münster. That's a town in North Rhine-Westfalia in the western part of Germany.

_____ you what the town is famous for. Then I'm going to tell you about my family, the area where I live and why I'm here. _____ take about three minutes.

_____ what my hometown is famous for. In 1648 Münster played an important role in the peace after the Thirty Years war. Today it has one of the largest universities in Germany. Most people go by bike in the city centre. _____ the Prinzipalmarkt, a street with a lot of old houses and buildings which were mainly rebuilt after World War II. _____ at the old cathedral nearby also made from sandstone which came from a forest in the area called Teutoburger Wald. Well, _____ that Münster is a fascinating city.

_____ my family. My father is from India and my mother is German. I have two sisters. One is older than me and studies engineering. The other one is only four years old and goes to kindergarten. We live not far from the Aasee, the biggest lake in Münster, and I go to a grammar school which was named after a famous 19th century writer from Münster, Annette von Droste-Hülshoff …

Üben

6 Englisch sprechen

Übung 4

 Choose one of the topics and make a mind map for a presentation.

1. You are going to make a presentation about what you have already learnt about the United States for your bilingual geography class.

2. Imagine you spent your summer holidays in New York. Tell your English class about your time there. Don't forget to talk about your feelings.

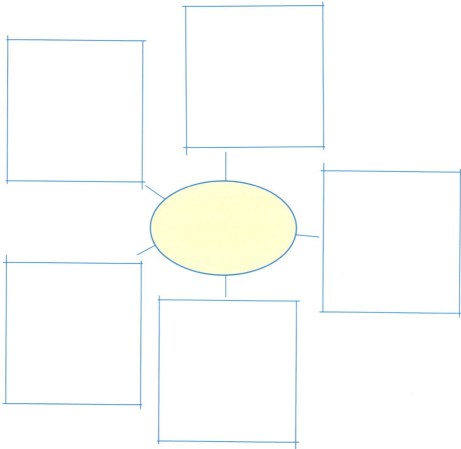

Übung 5

What is the "rule of six"? Choose the correct answer.

- [ ] Use a maximum of six lines and six words per slide.
- [ ] Remember the six steps how to make a good presentation.
- [ ] Practise your presentation in front of six people before you are well prepared.
- [ ] Remember: A good presentation does not take more than six minutes.

Üben

6 Englisch sprechen

Übung 6

Read the text and find a title for it.

The origin of Thanksgiving traces back to the 16th century when European immigrants and Native Americans shared a feast of turkey for the fall harvest. Turkeys, which are originally American birds, began appearing on dinner plates across the country after President Lincoln made Thanksgiving a national holiday in 1863. Every November since 1947, a "National Thanksgiving Turkey" has been presented to the U.S. President in the White House. Harry Truman got the first one. What is special about this ritual? This one turkey gets pardoned by the president every year. This means that it will not be killed and eaten. Thanksgiving is celebrated on the last Thursday of November in the US. Today it's not so much a harvest festival but the most important family day. Families come together on this day and eat roast turkey with side dishes such as sweet potatoes, peas or pumpkin and apple tart for dessert. Canada has its own Thanksgiving tradition, but they celebrate it in October.

_____

Übung 7

Highlight the most important information/keywords in the text.

Übung 8

Note down three key facts with a short note. Don't forget to use your own words!

Übung 9

Choose the first key information/aspect and write a text for your slide about it in your exercise book.

Üben

6 Englisch sprechen

Übung 10

 Often you have to explain something in a presentation. Practise this by giving an explanation for the following words in English. Try to use no more than one sentence.

Thanksgiving

to get detention

cell phone

subway

green card

homecoming

Wissen

6 Englisch sprechen

6.2 Argumentieren

Diskutieren ist ein wichtiger Bestandteil des Schul- wie auch des Berufsalltags später. Auch im Englischunterricht wird diese Fähigkeit im Verlauf der Mittelstufe immer wichtiger. Du lernst einen Standpunkt zu vertreten, einer anderen Meinung zuzustimmen oder ihr zu widersprechen. Dazu benutzt du wie im Deutschen bestimmte Redewendungen *(useful phrases)*.

Überlege dir deinen Standpunkt zum Thema und mache dir ggf. kurze Notizen zu verschiedenen Aspekten (nenne z. B. Fakten oder Beispiele), die für und/oder gegen die zu diskutierende Fragestellung sprechen, und trage ein wichtiges Argument vor.	It's a fact that smoking is not healthy. About 15 per cent of all humans die because of smoke or smoking.
Sag deine Meinung.	In my opinion smoking should/should not be allowed.
Hör zu, ob dein Gegenüber diese Meinung teilt oder nicht, um im Anschluss ggf. ein Gegenargument zu liefern.	I'm not sure about that. My grandmother is a heavy smoker and she is 80 now.
Geh auf dein Gegenüber ein. Nenne deine Argumente und drücke dabei Zustimmung oder Ablehnung aus.	I doubt that very much. I think so too.
Involviere dabei dein Gegenüber. Verwende dazu *question tags* (Bestätigungsfragen) und Nachfragen.	I already mentioned that smoking also causes many illnesses, <u>didn't I?</u> I didn't get that. Can you repeat your last point?
Mache deinen Standpunkt am Ende noch einmal klar und wiederhole dein wichtigstes Argument.	To sum up let me repeat that one in seven people worldwide die from smoking.
Versuche mit deinem Gegenüber eine Lösung oder einen Kompromiss zu finden.	Can we meet halfway?
Verwende übliche Redewendungen, die du auch aus dem Deutschen kennst, um deinen Standpunkt zu verdeutlichen:	
stating your opinion	I think/believe/feel …
agreeing	I agree./Exactly./I think so too. …
disagreeing	I disagree (completely)./I doubt that. …
Merke: Bleibe immer sachlich und höflich. Vermeide Einwortsätze wie *Yes.* und *No.*	~~That's rubbish!~~

Üben

6 Englisch sprechen

Übung 11

 Wrong one out. Cross out the useful phrase which doesn't fit.

Personnally I think … – Well, I'd say … – If you ask me … – I'm not convinced that …

I agree … – In my opinion … – Exactly! – I disagree completely!

I'm afraid I don't quite agree … – I doubt that. – I think so too. – I don't think that's a good idea.

Can you give me an example? – Could you explain that? – Sorry, I didn't catch that. – Can you repeat it?

Hi … – Dear classmates … – Ladies and gentlemen … – Thank you.

Übung 12

 Read the following discussion between Max and his American uncle Salman who are on a trip to New York. They are trying to agree on a sight for the day. Put the dialogue into the correct order.

Max: "Okay. Let's do it that way." **A**

Salman: "I'm certain that you would enjoy this one. Can we meet halfway? If we go to the Statue of Liberty right away, we could spend the afternoon in Central Park in case it will get terribly hot." **B**

Salman: "Sorry, son. I don't agree with you. It will probably be damn hot today. We could go for a walk and stay out of the sun under the trees. And don't forget we'd have to take the ferry to get to the Statue of Liberty." **C**

Max: "Central Park? Puhhh. Couldn't we go and see the Statue of Liberty instead? We could take fantastic pictures there. Central Park is not cool at all." **D**

Salman: "How do you feel about spending the day in Central Park? It's close by. We could rent a boat and enjoy the lake there." **E**

Max: "You've got a point, but there is nothing special about parks." **F**

A	B	C	D	E	F

Üben

6 Englisch sprechen

Übung 13

Make the following statements more polite.

"No, that's complete rubbish! I want to go to the Statue of Liberty."

"That sounds great but …
_____
_____
_____

"Parks aren't cool!"

_____
_____
_____

"Go to Central Park if you must. I will wait for you in our hotel."

_____
_____
_____

Übung 14

In English, please! Was sagst du (höflich), wenn du sagen willst …

… dass es dir leidtut, zu unterbrechen, aber dass du den Bus bekommen musst?

_____

… dass du schon erwähnt hast, dass deine Eltern dich heute Abend anrufen werden?

_____

… dass du die Idee wirklich magst, an eurer Schule nur noch mit Computern und iPads zu arbeiten.

_____

… dass du anderer Meinung bist, weil es dir mehr Spaß macht, das MOMA in New York zu besuchen statt Ellis Island.

_____
_____

… dass ihr einen Kompromiss finden solltet?

_____

Testen

6 Englisch sprechen

Klassenarbeit 1
 45 Minuten

Aufgabe 1

What can you say when you want to talk about the structure of your presentation? Tick the correct boxes.

- [ ] Can everyone hear me?
- [ ] First I'm going to talk about …
- [ ] Today I'd like to talk about the following topic.
- [ ] You will get a handout after my presentation.
- [ ] I have divided the presentation into three parts.
- [ ] At the end I had the problem that …
- [ ] Just give me a sign if you have a question.
- [ ] How does this topic actually relate to you?
- [ ] Please interrupt me if anything is unclear to you.

Aufgabe 2

Read part of the discussion between two Canadian friends and complete the words.

Pablo: "So what kind of film would you prefer to watch tonight?"

Brad: "I particu_____ like hor_____ films. What ab_____ you?"

Pablo: "Gosh no. I'm mo___ into rom_____ comedies. There is o____ on at the mom_____ with an act_____ I really li_____. It's Jennifer Lop_____. She can pl_____ almost any ro_____, can't she?"

Brad: "Abso_____. She is amaz_____! However, I'd pre_____ to see something with a lot of act_____ and spe_____ effects. What about this fi_____? The story is set in New Orleans and there is even a love story … "

Testen
6 Englisch sprechen

Aufgabe 3

 Read the presentation. What did Isabelle do well? What did she forget? Note at least three aspects each.

Hi. My name is Isabelle. I'm here to talk about my year in New Orleans. In the first part I'm going to give you some information about my host family. Then I'm going to describe my school life at high school. In the third part I'm going to mention the biggest differences between life in the US and my life here in Germany. At the end you will get information about who coordinates the exchange at our school.

Now where did I live? I shared a small apartment with my host family outside of New Orleans. You can see them here: Jack, Honor and their daughter Deborah. I got up at 6:30 and took the school bus. In America school buses are needed because in many cities there are only a few bus lines and railroads and no subway. This leads me to my second part: school life.

I attended the International High School, a multicultural school downtown with about 2000 students. First thing I did every weekday was go to my locker and get my books and notebooks. As teachers have their own room, you have to change rooms quite a lot. When you are only seconds late for class you already get a tardy, which means that your host parents are told that you were late. After three tardies you get detention.

Every morning we had to take the Pledge of Allegiance. I'll quickly write this on the board. Let me explain what this expression means: everyone stands, faces the American flag and puts the right hand over his or her heart. It is a ritual where you say that you will always be loyal to your country. At the start I had problems understanding some of my teachers but I didn't get bad grades. In school teachers speak most of the time. Students often just have to listen. The school spirit was amazing. One of the reasons for this probably is that you can join many different clubs in the afternoon. I played soccer a lot.

This brings me to my third point.

I'd like to finish by saying that I very much enjoyed my time in New Orleans. I did become a bit homesick but then I made new friends and even went on vacation with my host family. Hopefully my English is a lot better now, too.

If you are interested in a school year abroad, there will be a meeting in January. Just send an email to Ms Adam.

I hope I haven't forgotten anything?

Testen

6 Englisch sprechen

Aufgabe 4 What question would you have liked to ask her afterwards?

_____

Aufgabe 5 Now underline the keywords and write three prompt cards you could use to do the presentation yourself.

Testen

6 Englisch sprechen

Klassenarbeit 2
 45 Minuten

Aufgabe 6

Which of the following useful phrases can you use to express an opinion? Tick the correct boxes.

- [ ] Well, I'd say …
- [ ] We are of the opinion …
- [ ] It's a fact that …
- [ ] To sum up I'd like to say …
- [ ] Personally, I think …
- [ ] Let me give you an example.

Aufgabe 7

Write down three common **(weit verbreitete)** mistakes a presenter can make.

_____

_____

_____

Aufgabe 8

Give your opinion on the following statements. Do you (dis)agree? Say why! Use a different useful phrase each time.

There is still a lot of discrimination against minorities in the US.

_____

_____

Hollywood films are more interesting than German films.

_____

_____

London is cooler than New York.

_____

_____

Testen

6 Englisch sprechen

Sports competitions at school are worse than having normal lessons.
_____
_____

I would prefer to go to Canada than go to the US for a holiday with my parents.
_____
_____

Aufgabe 9

Driver's licence for teens or not? Kim from Cologne is in Kansas for a year where teenagers are allowed to drive a car as soon as they turn 14. Write a dialogue between Kim and her 14-year-old American boyfriend Jonathan. You can use the keywords for arguments from the box on the left. Don't forget to include all the useful phrases from the box on the right!

status symbol – stay fit because of more cycling or walking – to feel more independent – higher risk of accident or injury – to practise with parents – long distances …	Do you really think so? If you ask me, … You're quite right. You have a point there, but … Maybe we have to agree to disagree.

_____
_____
_____
_____
_____
_____
_____
_____
_____

Stichwortfinder

A

Adjektiv 38, 42, 110
adverbial clause 106, 108, 110, 113, 201
Adverbialsatz 106, 108, 110, 113, 201
agree 231 ff.
Argumentation 231 ff.
argumentieren 231 ff.
Artikel 10, 11, 15, 17, 28
as … as in Vergleichen 38
Aussprache 10, 130, 132

B

Bedingungssatz (Typ I, II und III) 87, 92, 94, 96, 113
Befehl 171
bestimmter Artikel 15, 28
by-agent 140

C

can 74, 76, 90, 175
clause of time 106, 113
collective noun 11
conditional 87 ff.
contact clause 186
could 76, 90, 175
countable noun 10

D

defining relative clause 186
direktes Objekt 141
direkte Rede 166, 167
disagree 231
Diskussion 231
each other / one another 28

E

Eigenname 15
Ersatzform der Hilfsverben 76, 79, 81, 152

F

fictional text 208
for 51, 52, 54
Frage 74, 79, 92, 96, 123, 146, 155, 171, 198, 210, 213, 217, 219, 231
future 61, 64, 87, 89, 152, 155, 156, 166

G

Gegenargument 231 ff.
Gerundium 193, 194, 198, 202
going to-future 61, 155, 166
Gruppenbezeichnung 11

H

Hilfsverb 74 ff.
Hörverstehen 124, 219

I

if-Satz 87, 92, 94, 96, 113
indirekte Frage 171
indirekte Rede 81, 164 ff.
indirektes Objekt 141
Infinitivkonstruktion 152, 198
Inhaltsangabe 213
irregular verb 55, 56

K

Komparativ 38
Konjunktion 87, 106, 113, 164
keyword 123, 208, 213

L

Lautschrift 130
literarischer Text 217

M

may 74, 76, 79, 175
might 79, 92, 96, 175
mind map 120
modal auxiliary 74 ff., 87, 89, 90, 152, 175
modales Hilfsverb 74 ff., 87, 89, 90, 152, 175
must 74, 76, 79, 81, 152, 175
mustn't 74, 76, 79, 175

N

Nebensatz 57, 87, 92, 96, 106 ff.
needn't 74, 175
nicht notwendiger Relativsatz 186
nicht zählbares Substantiv 10
Nomen 10, 11, 28, 42, 194, 201
non-defining relative clause 186
non-fictional text 208
not as / so … so in Vergleichen 38
notwendiger Relativsatz 186

O

Objekt 24, 110, 111, 140, 141, 146, 149, 152, 186, 193, 194, 198
Objektergänzung *(object complement)* 111
one / ones (prop-word) 28, 30
one another / each other 28
ought to 74, 79, 175

Stichwortfinder

P

Paarwort 11
pair noun 11
Partizipialkonstruktion 201
Partizip Perfekt 155, 201
Partizip Präsens 201
Passiv 81, 140 ff.
past participle 146, 149, 152, 155, 156
past perfect 57, 96, 149, 156, 166, 167
past progressive 49, 146, 156
past tense 49, 76, 81, 146, 166, 213
persönliches Passiv 144
Personalpronomen 164, 165
Plural der Substantive 10, 11
Präposition 111, 141, 146, 149, 186, 194
present participle 51, 57, 201
present perfect 51, 52, 54, 89, 149, 155, 166
present progressive 49, 64, 89, 140, 155
present tense 49, 113, 140, 166, 213
Präsentation 225 ff.
präsentieren 225 ff.
presentation 225 ff.
Pronomen 11, 28, 30
prop-word 28, 30

R

reciprocal pronoun 28
reflexive pronoun 24, 28
reflexives Verb 26
Reflexivpronomen 24, 28
Relativpronomen 186
Relativsatz 186, 201
reported speech 164 ff.
reporting verb 164
reziprokes Pronomen 28

S

Sachtext 208, 213, 215
Satzverkürzung 193 ff.
say (indirekte Rede) 164, 166
-self / -selves (Pronomen) 24
shall 74, 79, 175
should 74, 79, 90, 175
simple past 49, 57, 76, 92, 146, 156
simple present 49, 74, 87, 140, 155
since 51, 52, 54, 106, 107, 110, 113, 201
Sprechen 225 ff., 231 ff.
Steigerung 38
Stützwort *one / ones* 28, 30
Substantiv 10, 11, 28, 42, 194, 201
summary 213

T

Temporalsatz 106, 113
Textsorte 123
Textverständnis 123
than in Vergleichen 38
timetable future 64

U

unbestimmter Artikel 11, 15, 17
uncountable noun 10
unpersönliches Passiv 144

V

Verb 26, 49 ff., 74 ff., 87 ff., 140 ff., 164 ff.
Verbot 74, 76, 79
Vergleiche mit Adjektiven 38
Verneinung 74, 76, 150

W

W-Frage 210, 213,
while 106, 113, 201
will als Modalverb 74, 152
will-future 61, 87, 89, 152, 155, 166
Wörterbuch 130, 208
Wortfeld 120, 123, 124
Wortschatz 120
would 79, 90, 92, 94, 96, 156, 166, 175

Z

zählbares Substantiv 10, 28
Zeitformen des Verbs 26, 49 ff., 74 ff., 87 ff., 140 ff., 164 ff.
Zeitverschiebung 167, 171